TEXAS BUCKET LIST

Set Off on **150 Epic Adventures** and Discover Incredible Destinations to Live Out Your Dreams While Creating Unforgettable Memories that Will Last a Lifetime.

(Online Digital MAP included - access it through the link provided in the MAP Chapter of this book)

BeCrePress Travel

TEXAS BUCKET LIST

Table of Contents

TEXAS BUCKET LIST

TEXAS BUCKET LIST

INTRODUCTION

Welcome to the ultimate guide to the most beautiful destinations in Texas!

This book has been designed to provide a comprehensive overview of 150 of the best places to visit in the Lone Star State. Each destination has been carefully chosen based on its unique features, natural beauty, historical significance, and cultural relevance.

The book is structured to provide all the relevant information you need to plan your trip, and you can enjoy your trip in Texas. For each destination, you will find a detailed description of what to expect, including information on the address, which major city it is near, driving directions to get there, the best time to visit, any costs associated with seeing, and GPS coordinates. This information is handy, especially for those who plan to visit remote destinations.

The book is divided into forty-seven chapters based on the geographical zones of Texas. Each chapter covers a specific region of the state and provides an overview of the destinations within that region. The structure makes it easy to plan a trip around a particular state area or explore multiple zones on a more extended trip.

In addition to the detailed descriptions of each destination, the book also includes a bonus interactive map. This map comprises all 150 destinations featured in the book, making exploring the state quickly without wasting time looking for destinations on physical maps or in complicated apps.

So, whether you are a first-time visitor to Texas or a seasoned traveler, this book is an essential guide to the state's best destinations. Explore the natural wonders, historical landmarks, and cultural treasures that make Texas a truly unique and unforgettable destination.

ABOUT TEXAS

To access the Digital Map, please refer to the 'Map Chapter' in this book

Introduction

Texas is a famous tourist attraction state in the United States. It is known for its remarkable history, diverse culture, and unique geography worldwide. It is one of the most fascinating places in the United States. From cowboys and oil rigs to spicy Tex-Mex cuisine and NASA's Mission Control Center, there are plenty of reasons why Texas stands out from other states. This chapter will grab all the necessary information about Texas.

Importance of Texas in the United States

Texas is famous for its economy. It is among the second-largest state in the United States. The state is a hub for oil production, technology, aerospace, agriculture, and tourism.

Texas is known for its rich cultural history that tells the story to tourists. It was home to Native American tribes such as the Comanche and Apache before European explorers arrived in 1519. Texas imparts in Mexico's fight for independence from Spain.

The state became independent from Mexico after winning the famous Battle of San Jacinto during its revolution in 1836. It led to Texas becoming an independent republic until joining the United States nine years later as its 28th state.

It is the hub of cowboys and oil wells; Texas has many world-renowned universities, such as Rice University and The University of Texas at Austin. The city of Houston has NASA's Johnson Space Center. It trains astronauts for a space missions.

Because of its location on the Gulf Coast, thriving economy across diverse industries with distinct cultures – whether you're looking for cowboy boots or global cuisine – makes Texas an essential part of American identity today.

Geography

Texas almost covers an area of approximately 268,820 square miles. Four other states and Mexico border it to the south. The geography of Texas varies significantly due to its size and diverse landscapes.

East of Texas consists of rolling hills, forests, and numerous rivers, like the Sabine and Trinity. The central region consists mainly of grasslands and farmland used for agricultural production. In contrast, West Texas features a desert landscape with dramatic canyons like the Palo Duro Canyon.

Texas has some sights of water attractions, including Lake Texoma, Caddo Lake, and Amistad Reservoir. Tourists can enjoy boating and fishing here.

Moreover, it has some remarkable landforms, such as Big Bend National Park, which showcases stunning mountain ranges like Sierra Del Carmen Mountains and natural hot springs at Balmorhea State Park.

Overall, Texas' diverse geography offers something unique for everyone, whether you're seeking adventure in nature or looking to experience different cultures.

Landforms and natural resources

Texas boasts a diverse landscape that includes plains, mountains, forests, and coastlines. The state's geography characterizes by vast prairies in the north and west regions. These are home to ranches and farms producing cotton, wheat, and corn.

The eastern part of Texas has dense forests with oak trees and pines, while central Texas is hilly terrain dotted with limestone cliffs. The Trans-Pecos region in West Texas consists of mountain ranges, including the Davis Mountains, which offer hiking trails for outdoor enthusiasts.

Texas has abundant natural resources such as oil, natural gas, timber, and minerals, including iron ore and lignite coal. Its coastal waters support commercial fishing activities, with shrimp being one of the most highly sought-after seafood harvested from here.

In addition to its agricultural produce like beef cattle production and various crops grown throughout the state each year, Texas' vast oil reserves have made it an economic powerhouse within the US and globally. Overall, Texas' landforms and natural resources provide a rich foundation for industry and agriculture.

Native American tribes and settlements

Native American tribes and settlements played a significant role in the history of Texas. The region was home to various indigenous groups, including Comanche, Apache, Karankawa, Caddo, and many others. These tribes had distinct cultures and lifestyles and were well-adapted to their environment.

The Comanches were known for their horseback riding skills and hunting prowess, while the Karankawas were skilled fishermen who lived along the Gulf Coast. The Caddos built complex societies with elaborate trade networks that spanned present-day Texas, Louisiana, Arkansas, and Oklahoma.

These Native American communities relied on natural resources such as rivers and forests for survival. They also traded goods with European settlers who arrived later on in history.

Unfortunately, as more Europeans migrated into Texas territory throughout the 19th century, these native populations declined due to conflicts over land ownership and disease epidemics brought by outside settlers.

Today many Texans still pay tribute to these native communities' rich legacy through cultural festivals celebrating their traditions.

Spanish colonization

Spanish arrived here in the 16th century in what is now Texas. These explorers mainly searched for gold and silver but aimed to spread Christianity throughout the region. The first permanent settlement was established near El Paso in 1598 by Juan de Oñate.

The arrival of the Spanish brought significant changes to Texas. They introduced new animals, such as horses and cattle, which became vital to the economy for centuries. Additionally, they built missions and presidios (forts) throughout the region, serving as centers for religious conversion and military control.

However, their expansion into native lands often led to conflicts with indigenous tribes, who saw them as threatening their way of life. These tensions culminated in several revolts against Spanish rule, including the Pueblo Revolt of 1680.

Despite these challenges, Spanish colonization profoundly impacted Texas's culture and society. It laid the foundation for future development while creating lasting legacies still visible today through architectural styles like adobe buildings or the famous San Antonio Missions National Historical Park.

Spanish colonization left an indelible mark on Texas history that can still be seen today through its rich cultural heritage and historical landmarks scattered across this vast state!

Mexican rule and the Texas Revolution

Mexican rule and the Texas Revolution mark a significant turning point in the history of Texas. The region was initially under Spanish influence, but by 1821, Mexico had become independent from Spain and gained control over Texas. However, tensions soon arose between Mexico's government and Anglo-American settlers who migrated to Texas for fertile land.

The conflict escalated when Mexican President Antonio López de Santa Anna abolished the country's constitution and centralized power in his own hands. This move outraged Texans, who wanted more autonomy for their state. In 1835, Texans rose against Mexican authority with an army led by Sam Houston.

Texan forces won the initial battles at Gonzales, Goliad, and San Antonio before suffering defeat at The Alamo mission that same year which saw all defenders, including Davy Crockett, killed after they refused to surrender despite being heavily outnumbered.

However, the tide turned in favor of Texans at San Jacinto on April 21st, where they defeated Santa Anna's army capturing him personally as a prisoner, thus leading to recognition of independence for the Republic of Texas nine years later in 1845.

The legacy of this revolution can still be seen today through cultural celebrations such as Cinco de Mayo which commemorates Mexico's victory over French troops in Puebla; it also celebrates Hispanic heritage across America while highlighting Mexican-American contributions throughout US history.

Statehood and the Civil War

It became part of the United States in 1845 officially. However, its entrance into the Union was subject to controversy. The issue of slavery had been contentious for years, leading to Texas seceding from the Union in 1861 and joining the Confederacy during the Civil War.

Texas played a significant role in Confederate and Union efforts during the war. Many Texans fought for the Confederacy, including some famous names such as General Robert E. Lee's right-hand man, John Bell Hood.

However, many Texans remained loyal to the Union and fought against their fellow Southerners. This division caused much tension within families and communities throughout Texas.

The Civil War devastated many parts of Texas, particularly along its border with Mexico, where battles were frequent. Reconstruction after the war was also tricky for Texas, with tensions remaining high between those who supported slavery and those who did not.

Statehood and Civil War marked a significant period of change for Texas that would shape its future development as part of America's southern region.

20th-century developments, including the oil and gas industry

It marked a significant period of growth and development for Texas, particularly with the rise of the oil and gas industry. During this time, Texas cemented its position as one of America's primary energy producers.

The discovery of Spindletop in 1901 sparked an oil rush to East Texas, forever changing the state's economy. Wealth poured into Houston, Dallas-Fort Worth, San Antonio, and Austin bringing unprecedented growth to these cities. The abundance of natural resources also led to tremendous advances in technology and infrastructure across the state.

Texas became home to many large companies such as ExxonMobil, Shell Oil Company, and Marathon Petroleum Corporation, which invested heavily in research & development, leading to technological advancements like hydraulic fracturing or 'fracking.'

With their investments came jobs for Texans, earning them higher incomes than ever.

Despite fluctuations in global demand over time due to various reasons like recession periods or wars, overall investment has remained strong throughout modern history, ensuring continued economic stability for the region.

Culture and Society

Texas is a diverse and vibrant state with a rich culture and society. With a population of over 29 million people, Texas is the second-most populous state in the US after California. It's major cities and urban areas, including Houston, Dallas, Austin, and San Antonio, are centers of industry, innovation, and culture. Texas is known for its delicious cuisine, including Tex-Mex, barbecue, and Southern comfort food. The state is also renowned for its music and arts scenes, ranging from country and blues to theater and contemporary art. Sports and recreation are also significant aspects of Texas culture, with popular activities including football, basketball, rodeo, and hunting. Texas also has several professional sports teams, including the Dallas Cowboys and the Houston Astros. Overall, Texas culture and society are a dynamic blend of diverse influences and traditions, making the state a unique and exciting place to live and visit.

Government and Policies

The government and politics of Texas are unique and complex, reflecting the state's size, diversity, and history. Texas has a strong tradition of state and local governance, with a structure that includes a bicameral legislature, an executive branch headed by the governor, and a judicial branch consisting of elected judges and appointed justices. Political history in Texas shaped such as the state's frontier heritage, its history of segregation and racism, and its strong tradition of individualism and self-reliance. In the last few decades, Texas transferred to a solid republic state. Significant issues and debates in Texas today include immigration, education, healthcare, and voting rights, with some of the most contentious debates centering around race and social justice issues. Texas's government and politics reflect the state's unique character and history and continue to shape the state's future direction and identity.

Economy

Texas has a strong economy with industries and many sectors. Significant enterprises and corporations run in Texas, including technology, healthcare, and finance. Dell, American Airlines, and ExxonMobil are the most famous, headquartered in the state. Agriculture plays a pivotal role in Texas's economy. While the energy sector, including oil and gas, is a hub of the Texas economy. The state is the US's leading crude oil and natural gas producer. Texas also has a solid international trade presence, with trade partners including Mexico, Canada, China, and Japan. The state's ports, including the Port of Houston, are significant hubs for global trade, and the state's infrastructure and workforce make it an attractive location for businesses and investors. The Texas economy is a complex and dynamic system essential to the state's continued growth and prosperity.

Tourist Attractions

When you visit Texas, it offers a lot to tourists. Major cities in Texas, including Houston, Dallas, Austin, and San Antonio, provide enchanting tourist places, such as museums, shopping, and dining. Big Bend National Park is known for its stunning desert landscapes and scenic hiking trails. Cultural and historical landmarks, including The Alamo and San Antonio Missions, are also must-see destinations for history buffs and culture enthusiasts. Beaches and coastal attractions, such as South Padre Island, offer a chance to relax and enjoy the sunshine while offering various water sports and activities. You can enjoy several outdoor activities, like hiking, fishing, and hunting. If you are a wildlife lover, you may see many national parks. Whether you're interested in history, culture, or outdoor adventure, Texas has something to offer everyone.

Weather

The climate of Texas is primarily warm and sunny. However, the state's size and diverse geography mean significant variations in temperature depending on location. Coastal areas are generally more humid and prone to thunderstorms, while the western part of the state is arider, and drought-prone—seasonal weather significantly impacts Texas. In summer, the temperature often exceeds 90 degrees Fahrenheit in many areas. In winter, temperatures can be below-freezing in some regions. Spring and fall are mostly mild and pleasant, with comfortable temperatures and lower humidity. Texas is also prone to natural hazards such as hurricanes and tornadoes, particularly in coastal and eastern regions of the state. As a tourist, it is necessary to follow all the precautions to ensure your safety. Texas enjoys mainly warmth and sunshine, so it depends a lot on the time of visit.

Conclusion

Texas is a strong economy, remarkable history, and fantastic culture. Texas offers something for everyone, from its natural beauty and outdoor activities to its cultural and historic landmarks and urban centers. It is a beautiful blend of Mexican influence and Western heritage. The state faces multiple issues like the economy, climate change, and political issues. But yet, it is a land of opportunities

DALLAS

1. Dallas Zoo

Dallas Zoo is a 106-acre zoological park in southern Dallas, Texas. It is home to over 2,000 animals representing 406 species. It is the home of African elephants, lions, giraffes, primates, birds, reptiles, and aquatic animals.

The zoo provides an excellent environment for both its animal residents and its visitors. It offers a range of interactive experiences, like educational exhibits, behind-the-scenes tours, and animal encounters that allow visitors to learn about the animals and their habitats.

Dallas Zoo features a range of attractions, like the monorail, a carousel, a petting zoo, and dining options. The zoo offers a variety of events and programs, including summer camps, nighttime safari tours, and holiday-themed activities.

Location: Dallas Zoo at 650 S. R.L. Thornton Freeway (I-35E), Dallas, TX 75203, United States.

Closest City or Town: Irving, Grand Prairie, Mesquite, and Richardson.

How to Get There: You can access it in multiple ways.

It all depends on your location and preferred mode of transportation:

1. Driving visitors can take I-35E and exit at Marsalis Avenue, then follow the signs to the zoo.
2. You can access Dallas Zoo by public transportation. You can take the DART (Dallas Area Rapid Transit) Red Line to the Dallas Zoo Station, which is located right outside the zoo entrance.
3. You can also use ride-sharing apps like Uber or Lyft or take a taxi to the zoo.
4. Dallas Zoo offers bike racks for visitors who arrive on two wheels.

GPS coordinates 32.7411° N, 96.81528° W

Best Time to Visit: September and November

Pass/Permit/Fees: Tickets range from $16 to $22. Children under the age of 2 are free.

Did you know? It is the home of eight magnificent African elephants.

2. Nasher Sculpture Center

Nasher Sculpture Center is a well-known museum about the contemporary sculpture of the Arts District of downtown Dallas, Texas. It carries a diverse collection of sculptures, including art by some of the world's most celebrated artists, such as Auguste Rodin, Pablo Picasso, and Richard Serra. The building is a work of art designed by architect Renzo Piano and features a stunning outdoor sculpture garden. The museum hosts a variety of exhibitions, programs, and events throughout the year, including lectures, tours, and workshops. The Nasher Sculpture Center is a treat to watch for lovers of contemporary art and sculpture.

Location: 2001 Flora St, Dallas, TX 75201, United States

Closest City or Town: Irving, Grand Prairie, Mesquite, and Richardson.

How to Get There: Multiple options can use to get into Nasher Sculpture Center.

1. Drivers can take the Dallas North Tollway or I-35E, exit at Woodall Rodgers Freeway, and follow the signs to the Arts District. Many paid parking is available.

2. DART (Dallas Area Rapid Transit) Red or Blue Line to the St. Paul Station, then walk a few blocks to the museum.

3. You can hire ride-sharing services like Uber, Lyft or a taxi to the museum.

4. Two wheels vehicle facility is also available here.

GPS coordinates: 32.7882° N, 96.8002° W

Best Time to Visit: Summer.

Pass/Permit/Fees: Tickets range from $5 to $10. Children at the age of 11 are free.

Did you know? It is the home of the fantastic artwork of Rodin, Brancusi, Matisse, Picasso, Koons, Calder, and Miró.

3. Reunion Tower

Reunion Tower is a beautiful landmark and observation tower in downtown Dallas, Texas. It stands 561 feet tall and is famous for its geodesic dome structure and display of colorful LED light shows at night. The tower was completed in 1978 as part of the Reunion

development project and has since become a popular tourist destination, offering breathtaking 360-degree sights from its view deck. Visitors can enjoy fine dining at the tower's rotating restaurant, Five Sixty, by Wolfgang Puck. Reunion Tower is not only a symbol of Dallas but also an important cultural and architectural icon of the United States.

Location: 300 Reunion Blvd E, Dallas, TX 75207, USA

Closest City or Town: Irving, Grand Prairie, Mesquite.

How to Get There: If you drive toward 300 Reunion Blvd E, Dallas, TX 75207, a paid parking garage is available on-site.

If you use public transportation, you can take the local DART (Dallas Area Rapid Transit) light rail to the Union Station stop, a short walk from the tower.

You can hire a ride service like Uber or Lyft to get to the tower.

Once you arrive at the tower, you can purchase tickets to the observation deck and make reservations for the restaurant. The observation deck and restaurant have separate entrances, so check which access suits your plans.

GPS coordinates: 32.7755° N, 96.8089° W

Best Time to Visit: Summer.

Pass/Permit/Fees: Tickets range from $24 to $40. Children at the age of 3 are free.

Did you know? The tower is famous for its location at 300 Reunion Boulevard in the Reunion district.

4. Perot Museum of Nature and Science

The Perot Museum of Nature and Science is a state-of-the-art museum. The museum features five floors of interactive exhibits that showcase the wonders of nature and science, including fossils, gems and minerals, space, engineering, and more. The museum also has a 3D theater, an outdoor science park, and a variety of hands-on activities for visitors of all ages. The museum's iconic architecture evokes the natural environment of Texas, with a stunning glass-encased escalator that provides panoramic views of the downtown skyline. The Perot Museum of Nature and Science is a must-visit destination for anyone interested in science, technology, engineering, and math (STEM) education and entertainment.

Location: 2201 N Field St, Dallas, TX 75201, USA

Closest City or Town: Arlington, Irving, Plano, and Garland.

How to Get There: The car drivers can go to 2201 N Field St, Dallas, TX 75201; a parking garage is available on-site for a fee.

You can utilize DART (Dallas Area Rapid Transit) light rail to the Akard Station, a short walk from the museum. You can also take a bus to the museum, with several bus routes serving the area.

Uber or Lyft's option is also available to get to the museum.

Once you arrive at the museum, you can purchase tickets to explore the exhibits and participate in various activities. The museum opens daily, with extended hours on different days, so you must check the hours of operation before planning your visit.

GPS coordinates: 32.7869° N, 96.8066° W

Best Time to Visit: Summer & Rainy day

Pass/Permit/Fees: Tickets range from $15 to $25. Children at the age of 1 are free.

Did you know? It is famous for its mesmerizing architecture.

5. The George W Bush Presidential Library and Museum

The George W. Bush Presidential Library and Museum are on the campus of Southern Methodist University in Dallas, Texas. The museum carries a collection of artifacts, documents, and photographs related to the presidency of George W. Bush, including exhibits on September 11, 2001, the wars in Afghanistan and Iraq, Hurricane Katrina, and the financial crisis of 2008. The museum also has a master copy of the Oval Office and a presidential limousine. The library is a research center for scholars and students, housing over 70 million pages of documents related to the Bush presidency. The George W. Bush Presidential Library and Museum offer a unique perspective on recent American history and politics.

Location: 2943 SMU Boulevard, Dallas, TX 75205, USA.

Closest City or Town: University Park, Highland Park, Richardson, Irving, Fort Worth.

How to Get There: You can easily access the museum by car as it is near several major highways, including US-75 and I-635. There is also plenty of parking available on the SMU campus.

1. Dallas Area Rapid Transit (DART) offers bus routes and light rail lines that stop near the SMU campus. The museum is also accessible via the Mustang Express Shuttle, a free shuttle service provided by SMU.

2. If you are flying in from out of town, the closest airport is Dallas Love Field, located approximately 7 miles from the museum. You can fly into Dallas/Fort Worth International Airport, about 20 miles away.

GPS coordinates: 32.8412° N, 96.7782° W

Best Time to Visit: Summer.

Pass/Permit/Fees: Tickets range from $6 to $20. Children at the age of 5 are free.

Did you know? It is famous for the presidency of George. Bush.

6. Dallas Arboretum & Botanical Gardens

The Dallas Arboretum & Botanical Gardens is a 66-acre oasis located on the eastern shore of White Rock Lake in Dallas, Texas. It is a stunning collection of botanical gardens and features over 20 themed gardens, including the Nancy Rutchik Red Maple Rill, the Rory Meyers Children's Adventure Garden, and the Woman's Garden. You can relax in a calm atmosphere and enjoy the breathtaking gardens and lake views. It hosts seasonal activities, like the famous Dallas Blooms Festival in the spring and the 12 Days of Christmas exhibit during the winter. With its beautiful landscapes and diverse plant collections, the Dallas Arboretum & Botanical Gardens is a must-visit destination for nature lovers and garden enthusiasts.

Location: 8525 Garland Rd, Dallas, TX 75218, USA

Closest City or Town: Irving, Mesquite.

How to Get There: Visitors can drive and park in the parking lot, which is located on-site.

Parking is free for members and $15 per vehicle for non-members.

1. Visitors can take the DART (Dallas Area Rapid Transit) bus or train to the White Rock Station, about a mile from the Arboretum. Visitors can take a taxi, Uber, or Lyft to the Arboretum.

2. The Arboretum is on the White Rock Trail, a popular cycling route. Visitors can bike to the Arboretum and park in the designated bike racks.

3. Visitors can also walk to the Arboretum from nearby neighborhoods or parks.

GPS coordinates: 32°49'17"N 96°43'3"W

Best Time to Visit: Spring.

Pass/Permit/Fees: Tickets range from $3 to $20. Children under the age of 5 are free.

Did you know? It is famous because of its stunning view and calm atmosphere.

7. The Sixth Floor Museum at Dealey Plaza

The Sixth Floor Museum at Dealey Plaza is in the Texas School Book Depository building in Dallas, Texas. The museum is preserving the legacy of President John F. Kennedy. Visitors can explore exhibits that chronicle JFK's life and presidency, the events leading up to his assassination, and the subsequent investigation. The museum's main attraction is the sixth-floor exhibit, which features artifacts, photographs, and multimedia displays that provide an in-depth look at the assassination and its aftermath. The museum guides tours and educational programs for visitors of all ages.

Location: 411 Elm St, Dallas, TX 75202, USA

Closest City or Town: Irving, Mesquite.

How to Get There: Visitors can drive to the museum and park in one of the nearest paid parking lots or garages. The closest parking garage is at 501 Elm Street, across from the museum's entrance.

1. Visitors can take the DART (Dallas Area Rapid Transit) bus or train to the West End Station, about a 10-minute walk from the museum. From the station, visitors can walk south on Houston Street to Elm Street and then turn right to reach the museum.

2. Visitors can bike to the museum and park their bicycles at the designated bike racks located on Elm Street.

3. Visitors staying in nearby hotels or attractions can walk to the museum. The museum is in the heart of downtown Dallas, within walking distance of many popular destinations.

GPS coordinates: 32.7798° N, 96.8085° W

Best Time to Visit: Summer, Winter.

Pass/Permit/Fees: Tickets range from $14 to $18. Children under the age of 5 are free.

Did you know? It is famous for the legacy of President John F. Kennedy.

8. Klyde Warren Park

Klyde Warren Park is a 5.2-acre urban area in the heart of downtown Dallas, Texas. The park builds over the Woodall Rodgers Freeway; It features a wide range of amenities for visitors, including a performance pavilion, a children's playground, a dog park, a walking and biking trail, and numerous food trucks and restaurants. The park offers various events and activities throughout the year, such as fitness classes, live music performances, and outdoor movie screenings. With its central location, stunning views of the Dallas skyline, and vibrant atmosphere, Klyde Warren Park has become a popular choice for locals and visitors alike.

Location: 2012 Woodall Rodgers Fwy, Dallas, TX 75201, USA

Closest City or Town: Irving, Mesquite.

How to Get There: Visitors can drive to the park and park in one of the nearest paid parking lots or garages. The area has many parking options, including the park's underground parking garage, accessible from either Pearl Street or Olive Street.

1. Visitors can take the DART (Dallas Area Rapid Transit) bus or train to the St. Paul Station.

2. Visitors can bike to the park and park their bicycles at the designated bike racks located throughout the park.

3. Visitors staying in nearby hotels or attractions can walk to the park. Klyde Warren Park is in the heart of downtown Dallas, within walking distance of many popular destinations.

GPS coordinates: 32.7894° N, 96.8016° W

Best Time to Visit: Summer, Spring.

Pass/Permit/Fees: Entry is free.

Did you know? It is famous for its beauty and playgrounds for kids and pets(dogs).

9. Dallas Museum of Art

The Dallas Museum of Art (DMA), a renowned art museum, is in the Arts District of downtown Dallas, Texas. The museum houses a vast and diverse collection of over 24,000 objects, from ancient artifacts to contemporary art pieces.

The museum's permanent collection includes works from various world regions, including Africa, Asia, Europe, and the Americas, and a significant collection of American art. The museum hosts numerous temporary exhibitions annually, showcasing various art movements and styles. With its exceptional collection, innovative programming, and commitment to accessibility, the Dallas Museum of Art is a must-see destination for art lovers visiting Dallas.

Location: 1717 N Harwood St, Dallas, TX 75201, USA

Closest City or Town: Garland, Plano.

How to Get There: Visitors can drive to the museum and park in the DMA parking garage at the corner of Ross Avenue and Harwood Street. Several paid parking lots and garages are in the surrounding area.

1. Visitors can take the DART (Dallas Area Rapid Transit) bus or train to St. Paul Station or Pearl Station within walking distance of the museum. Visitors can walk north on Pearl Street from the stations to the museum.

2. Visitors can bike to the museum and park their bicycles at the designated bike racks located on the Harwood Street side of the museum.

3. Visitors staying in the nearby hotels or attractions can walk to the museum.

GPS coordinates: 32.7877° N, 96.8010° W

Best Time to Visit: Whole Year

Pass/Permit/Fees: General Entry is free.

Did you know? It is famous for its global collection of Art.

10. White Rock Lake Park

White Rock Lake Park is an expansive urban park in eastern Dallas, Texas. The park covers over 1,015 acres and features a 9-mile trail that circles the scenic White Rock Lake. Visitors can enjoy various outdoor activities in the park, including biking, hiking, kayaking, fishing, and picnicking. The park has several amenities, including playgrounds, picnic areas, and a dog park. It is home to multiple wildlife, like birds, turtles, and fish, making it a popular destination for nature enthusiasts. With its natural beauty and diverse recreational opportunities, White Rock Lake Park is a favorite spot for locals and visitors.

Location: 8300 East Lawther Drive.

Closest City or Town: Addison, Balch Springs, Carrollton.

How to Get There: Visitors can drive to the park and park in one of the many parking lots located throughout the park. The park's main gate is Garland Road, just east of Buckner Boulevard.

1. Visitors can take the DART (Dallas Area Rapid Transit) bus to one of the stops located near the park, including the #60 and #428 buses. From there, visitors can walk or bike to the park.

2. Visitors can bike to the park and park their bicycles at the designated bike racks located throughout the park.

3. Visitors staying in nearby neighborhoods can walk to the park. The park has several pedestrian entrances, including those located at the intersection of Lawther Drive and Mockingbird Lane and near the Arboretum.

GPS coordinates: 32.8281° N, 96.7253° W

Best Time to Visit: April-June.

Pass/Permit/Fees: General Entry is free.

Did you know? It is famous for its various activities.

11. Dallas Cattle Drive Sculptures

The Dallas Cattle Drive Sculptures is a magnificent art installation in Dallas. It is a collection of 49 bronze statues depicting a cattle drive in the 19th century. The sculptures are spread across a 1.5-acre plaza and show cowboys herding longhorn cattle through a river, bridge, and hill.

The sculptures were created by the artist Robert Summers, inspired by the rich history of cattle drives in Texas in the late 1800s. The installation took five years to complete.

Visitors to the Dallas Cattle Drive Sculptures can enjoy the excitement and drama of a cattle drive, with the realistic depiction of cowboys on horseback, longhorn cattle, and the rugged terrain of the American West. It is a treat to watch for art lovers and history buffs visiting Dallas.

Location: 900 Jackson St, Dallas, TX 75202, United States.

Closest City or Town: Irving, Richardson.

How to Get There: You can use your car or rent one to get to the sculptures. Several parking options are available nearby, including metered street parking, parking garages, and surface lots.

1. You can take the Dallas Area Rapid Transit (DART) to the sculptures. The closest DART station is Akard Station, about a 10-minute walk from Pioneer Plaza.

2. You can also take a taxi or ride-sharing service like Uber or Lyft to get to the sculptures.

Once you arrive at Pioneer Plaza, the sculptures are throughout the plaza, so you can easily walk around and enjoy them. Admission to the sculptures is free, and there are no set visiting hours, as the park is open to the public 24/7.

GPS coordinates: 32.7813° N, 96.8054° W

Best Time to Visit: Summer, Winter.

Pass/Permit/Fees: General Entry is free.

Did you know? It is famous for its sculpture art. It is a must-visit place for art lovers.

12. NorthPark Center

NorthPark Center is a premier shopping destination in Dallas, Texas. Here, more than 235 retailers, including high-end fashion brands, restaurants, and entertainment options. The center also features a range of contemporary and modern art pieces. Here, you can experience the fantastic art of famous artists like Andy Warhol, Frank Stella, and Joel Shapiro. Visitors can experience shopping at designer boutiques to attending art exhibitions and cultural events. NorthPark Center has become a must-visit attraction for locals and tourists alike, known for its upscale ambiance, world-class amenities, and outstanding customer service.

Location: 8687 N Central Expy, Dallas, TX 75225, USA.

Closest City or Town: Garland, Irving, Richardson.

How to Get There: You can drive to North Park Center. The shopping center is an intersection of the North Central Expressway and Northwest Highway (Loop 12). It is easily accessible from major highways and thoroughfares.

1. You can go on Dallas Area Rapid Transit (DART) to get to North Park Center. The closest DART station is Park Lane Station, about a 10-minute walk from the shopping center.

2. You can easily hire a taxi or use Uber or Lyft to reach North Park Center.

Once you arrive at North Park Center, multiple parking options are available, including surface lots, garages, and valet parking. Additionally, the shopping center is accessible to visitors with disabilities, and there are designated parking spots and accessible entrances located throughout the property.

GPS coordinates: 32.8696° N, 96.7737° W

Best Time to Visit: Summer, Winter.

Pass/Permit/Fees: Tickets range from $5 to $10. Children at the age of 2 are free.

Did you know? It is a luxurious and high-fashion place.

13. Dallas Holocaust and Human Rights Museum

The Dallas Holocaust and Human Rights Museum is a world-class museum in downtown Dallas, Texas's West End Historic District. The museum preserves the memory of the Holocaust and other genocides and promotes human rights and social justice for all. The exhibits feature powerful artifacts, interactive displays, and personal testimonies from survivors, highlighting the atrocities committed during the Holocaust and other genocides throughout history. Visitors can also explore topics such as civil and human rights, the dangers of prejudice and discrimination, and the importance of taking action to promote social justice. The museum's mission is to engage people to stand against hate and intolerance and to work for a better world.

Location: 300 N Houston St, Dallas, TX 75202, USA

Closest City or Town: Garland, Irving.

How to Get There: You can use your car or rent one to visit the museum. There are several parking options available.

1. You can take the Dallas Area Rapid Transit (DART) to the museum. The closest DART station is the West End Station, located about a 5-minute walk from the museum.

2. You can also hire a taxi or use ride-sharing services.

GPS coordinates: 32.7808° N, 96.8079° W

Best Time to Visit: Summer, Winter.

Pass/Permit/Fees: Entry is free. But it is better to reserve tickets online.

Did you know? It aims to protect human rights and work for a better world.

14. Pioneer Plaza

Pioneer Plaza is a unique outdoor public space in downtown Dallas, Texas. The plaza features a larger-than-life bronze sculpture of a cattle drive, with over 70 individual bronze longhorn steers and three bronze cowboys on horseback, commemorating the city's rich history as a cattle industry hub—the sculpture amidst a beautiful park with walking paths, trees, and a flowing stream. Visitors can explore the sculptures up close, take photos, and learn about the area's history through interpretive panels throughout the plaza.

Location: 1428 Young St, Dallas, TX 75202, USA

Closest City or Town: Garland, Irving, Fort Worth.

How to Get There: You can use your car or rent one to get to Pioneer Plaza. The plaza is near the intersection of Young Street and Griffin Street, just off Interstate 35E.

1. You can take the Dallas Area Rapid Transit (DART) to Pioneer Plaza. The closest DART station is the West End Station, about a 10-minute walk from the plaza.

2. You can book a taxi or use a ride-sharing service.

GPS coordinates: 32.7766° N, 96.8012° W

Best Time to Visit: Summer, Winter.

Pass/Permit/Fees: Entry is free.

Did you know? The specialty of Pioneer Plaza is its larger-than-life bronze sculpture of a cattle drive.

15. Morton H Meyerson Symphony Center

The Morton H. Meyerson Symphony Center is a world-renowned concert hall located in Dallas, Texas. Famous architects I.M. Pei and acoustician Russell Johnson created a venue that would provide exceptional acoustics for classical music performances. The building features a striking asymmetrical exterior with curved forms and sweeping lines. At the same time, the interior boasts a spacious and elegant hall with 2,062 seats arranged in a fan-shaped configuration around the stage. The

Meyerson Symphony Center is home to the Dallas Symphony Orchestra and hosts various musical performances, from classical to contemporary. It is one of the finest concert halls in the world.

Location: 2301 Flora St, Dallas, TX 75201, USA

Closest City or Town: Garland, Irving.

How to Get There: If you are driving, the center is easily accessible via major highways like I-35E, I-30, and the Dallas North Tollway. Paid parking is available at the Lexus Silver Parking Garage adjacent to the center and several nearby lots and garages.

You can use Dallas Area Rapid Transit (DART) bus and rail routes, including the D-Link free shuttle service that runs through the arts district. The closest DART rail station is Pearl/Arts District, about a 10-minute walk from the center.

Finally, if you are staying in a downtown Dallas hotel, the center is likely within walking distance or a short ride on a ride-sharing service like Uber or Lyft.

GPS coordinates: 32.7899° N, 96.7986° W

Best Time to Visit: Throughout the year.

Pass/Permit/Fees: Different prices depend upon concerts.

Did you know? It is home to music concerts and attracts tourists with its beautiful architecture.

16. Bishop Arts District

The Bishop Arts District is a trendy and vibrant neighborhood in the Oak Cliff area of Dallas, Texas, USA. Once a sleepy commercial district, it has become a sign of shopping, dining, and entertainment. The neighborhood is known for its unique boutiques, art galleries, and eclectic restaurants serving a range of cuisines, from Tex-Mex to Italian to vegan. Tourists can enjoy live music, theater performances, and cultural events like art walks and street festivals. The Bishop Arts District is a must-visit destination for anyone looking for a fun and lively atmosphere with a unique and eclectic vibe.

Location: Dallas, TX 75208, USA

Closest City or Town: Glen Rose, Paris.

How to Get There: You can drive through I-35E or I-30 to the Bishop Arts District. There is also street parking available throughout the neighborhood.

While on public transportation, you can use the Dallas Area Rapid Transit (DART) rail system to the nearby Bishop Arts Station on the Oak Cliff streetcar line. You can also take a bus to Jefferson Boulevard at Bishop stop near the heart of the Bishop Arts District.

Finally, if you are staying in a downtown Dallas hotel, you can take a ride-sharing service like Uber or Lyft to reach the Bishop Arts District in about 10-15 minutes, depending on traffic.

GPS coordinates: 32.7473° N, 96.8304° W

Best Time to Visit: Spring, in the fall.

Pass/Permit/Fees: $25.

Did you know? It is famous for its diverse activities.

17. Frontiers of Flight Museum

The Frontiers of Flight Museum is an excellent destination for aviation enthusiasts and history buffs in Dallas, Texas, USA. The museum showcases a vast collection of aviation artifacts, aircraft, and spacecraft, from the Wright Flyer to modern commercial jets and military planes. Tourists can learn about the history of flight through interactive exhibits, including flight simulators, a planetarium, and a comprehensive collection of photographs and documents. The museum offers guided tours, educational programs, and special events. The Frontiers of Flight Museum is a fascinating and engaging experience for people of all ages, showcasing human flight's incredible history and technological advancements.

Location: 6911 Lemmon Ave, Dallas, TX 75209, USA.

Closest City or Town: Irving, Fort Worth.

How to Get There: You can reach the museum via significant highways like I-35E and the Dallas North Tollway by car. There is ample parking available on-site, including designated spaces for disabled visitors.

On public transportation, you can take the Dallas Area Rapid Transit (DART) bus route 529 to the Lemmon @ Willowbrook stop, a short walk from the museum.

Alternatively, you can take the DART rail system to Inwood/Love Field Station and transfer to bus route 529.

Finally, if you are staying in a downtown Dallas hotel, you can take a ride-sharing service like Uber or Lyft to reach the Frontiers of Flight Museum in about 15-20 minutes, depending on traffic.

GPS coordinates: 32.8421° N, 96.8358° W

Best Time to Visit: Throughout the year

Pass/Permit/Fees: Tickets range from $9 to $12. Children at the age of 2 are free.

Did you know? It is famous for items related to flight.

18. Dallas World Aquarium

The Dallas World Aquarium is a unique and exciting attraction in downtown Dallas, Texas, USA. The aquarium is home to diverse aquatic and land animals worldwide, including sharks, rays, sea turtles, and exotic birds. Visitors can explore various exhibits, such as the Orinoco - Secrets of the River, featuring river wildlife from South America, and the Mundo Maya, showcasing the biodiversity of the rainforests of Central and South America. Additionally, the aquarium offers interactive experiences, such as feeding and encountering live animals up close. The Dallas World Aquarium is a thrilling and educational experience for visitors of all ages.

Location: 1801 N Griffin St, Dallas, TX 75202, USA

Closest City or Town: Garland, Plano.

How to Get There: Driving, you can reach the aquarium via significant highways like I-35E and I-30. You may use paid parking in the lot adjacent to the aquarium.

On public transport, you will take the Dallas Area Rapid Transit (DART) rail system to the West End Station, a short walk from the aquarium. You can also take the free D-Link bus, which runs through downtown Dallas and stops near the aquarium.

Finally, if you are staying in a downtown Dallas hotel, you can take a ride-sharing service like Uber or Lyft to reach the Dallas World Aquarium in about 5-10 minutes, depending on traffic.

GPS coordinates: 32.7835° N, 96.8054° W

Best Time to Visit: Throughout the year.

Pass/Permit/Fees: Tickets range from $19 to $27.

Did you know? It is a must-see place for an aquatic lover.

GRAPEVINE

1. Grapevine Vintage Railroad

The Grapevine Vintage Railroad is an excellent train ride that takes visitors back in time, showcasing the beauty of Texas Hill Country. The train is located in Grapevine, Texas, USA, and offers various excursion packages, including stops at historic sites, wineries, and other attractions. A vintage steam or diesel locomotive pulls the train and features restored 1920s and 1930s-era coaches that glimpse the golden age of rail travel. The Grapevine Vintage Railroad is a unique and memorable experience that transports visitors to a bygone era and offers a fascinating perspective on the history of Texas.

Location: 707 S Main St, Grapevine, TX 76051, USA

Closest City or Town: Tarrant County, Fort Worth.

How to Get There: By car, you can reach the Grapevine Vintage Railroad via significant highways like I-35E and State Highway 114. Free parking is available at the Grapevine Vintage Railroad Depot, the starting point for all train excursions.

On public transportation, you can take the Dallas Area Rapid Transit (DART) rail system to the Trinity Mills Station in Carrollton and then transfer to the DCTA A-train, which stops at the Downtown Grapevine Station, located a short walk from the Grapevine Vintage Railroad Depot.

Finally, you can book a ride or taxi if you are staying in a downtown Dallas hotel.

GPS coordinates: 32.9338° N, 97.0780° W

Best Time to Visit: Throughout the year

Pass/Permit/Fees: Tickets range from $20 to $32.

Did you know? It is a treat to watch to witness the historical scenes.

2. Grapevine Historic Main Street District

The Grapevine Historic Main Street District is a charming and vibrant destination in Grapevine, Texas, USA. The district is famous for various shops, restaurants, and entertainment venues in restored historic buildings dating to the 19th and early 20th centuries. Visitors can explore the district's quaint streets and alleys, enjoy live music performances, and sample local cuisine and wines. The community also hosts numerous events throughout the year, such as the GrapeFest wine festival and the Main Street Fest arts and crafts festival. The Grapevine Historic Main Street District is a delightful destination showcasing Texas's rich history and culture.

Location: Grapevine, TX, USA.

Closest City or Town: Chandler, Lake of the Woods, Mettler.

How to Get There: Driving, you can reach the district via major highways like I-35E and State Highway 114. Ample free parking is available in various lots and garages throughout the district.

If you use public transportation, you can take the Dallas Area Rapid Transit (DART) rail system to the Trinity Mills Station in Carrollton, then transfer to the DCTA A-train, which stops at the Downtown Grapevine Station, located a short walk from the Main Street District.

Finally, if you are staying in a downtown Dallas hotel, you can book a ride. Grapevine Historic Main Street District in about 30-40 minutes, depending on traffic.

GPS coordinates: 32.9365° N, 97.0712° W

Best Time to Visit: Throughout the year.

Pass/Permit/Fees: General entry is free.

Did you know? It is a home of multiple entertainment activities.

FORT WORTH

1. Fort Worth Zoo

The Fort Worth Zoo is worldwide renowned in Fort Worth, Texas, founded in 1909. The zoo covers an area of 64 acres and is home to over 7,000 animals of 540 species. The zoo is famous for its collection of exotic animals, including gorillas, orangutans, tigers, and giraffes. It also features a variety of exhibits and habitats, such as the African Savannah, Asian Falls, and World of Primates. Visitors can also enjoy a range of attractions and experiences, such as the Texas Wild! Petting Corral, the Texas Nature Traders program, and the Yellow Rose Express Train. The Fort Worth Zoo is dedicated to conservation, education, and animal welfare and is a must-visit destination for animal lovers of all ages.

Location: 1989 Colonial Pkwy, Fort Worth, TX 76110, USA

Closest City or Town: Kennedale, Lake Worth, Blue Mound.

How to Get There: You can take I-30 and exit University Drive by car. From there, head south on University Drive and turn right onto Colonial Parkway. The zoo will be on your left.

1. The Fort Worth Zoo can access buses through the Trinity Metro transit system. Route 7 and Route 12 both have stops near the zoo. You can use the Trinity Metro website or mobile app to plan your trip and purchase tickets.

2. Uber and Lyft operate in Fort Worth, and you can use their apps to request a ride to the zoo.

3. Nearby people can use a bike or walk to the zoo. The Trinity Trails system runs near the zoo and provides a scenic route for those who prefer to travel by foot or bike.

GPS coordinates: 32.7232° N, 97.3564° W

Best Time to Visit: Spring & Summer.

Pass/Permit/Fees: Tickets range from $14 to $18. Children at the age of 2 are free.

Did you know? It is famous because of the various types of animals.

2. Fort Worth Stockyards National Historic District

The Fort Worth Stockyards National Historic District is a popular tourist destination in Fort Worth, Texas. The district spans 98 acres and has various shops, restaurants, museums, and entertainment venues celebrating the city's rich Western heritage. Visitors can watch live cattle drives, visit the Texas Cowboy Hall of Fame, attend a rodeo or bull-riding event at the Cowtown Coliseum, and shop for Western wear and souvenirs. The district is also home to the Fort Worth Herd, a group of longhorn cattle driven down Exchange Avenue twice daily. The Fort Worth Stockyards National Historic District is a must-visit destination for anyone interested in Western history, culture, and entertainment.

Location: 131 E Exchange Ave, Fort Worth, TX 76164, USA

Closest City or Town: Dallas, Irving, Plano.

How to Get There: As a car driver, you can take I-35W and exit onto NE 28th St/Northside Dr. From there, turn left onto N Main St and continue onto N Stockyards Blvd. The historic district will be on your right.

1. The Trinity Metro TEXRail commuter rail line has a station at the Fort Worth Stockyards, making it easy to get there from downtown Fort Worth or the Dallas/Fort Worth International Airport.

2. You can book a ride or taxi.

3. You can also bike or walk to the Stockyards. The Trinity Trails system runs near the Stockyards and provides a scenic route for those who prefer to travel by foot or bike.

GPS coordinates: 32°47'25"N, 97°20'46"W

Best Time to Visit: Spring & fall.

Pass/Permit/Fees: General entry is free.

Did you know? It is famous worldwide for its Western culture, with stockyards, cowboys, and rodeos.

3. Sundance Square

Sundance Square is a bustling entertainment district in downtown Fort Worth, Texas. It is a pedestrian-friendly area that spans 35 blocks and has restaurants, shops, theaters, and public art installations. One of the defining features of Sundance Square is the iconic 216-foot-tall Sundance Square Plaza, which hosts concerts, movies, and other events throughout the year. Visitors can also explore the Bass Performance Hall, a stunning venue for concerts and Broadway shows, or stroll through the Fort Worth Water Gardens, a peaceful oasis in the city's heart. Sundance Square is a lively destination with its festive atmosphere and diverse offerings.

Location: Sundance Square | Fort Worth, TX 76102-3105

Closest City or Town: Irving, Plano.

How to Get There: It is easily accessible by car, public transportation, or on foot. Car drivers, there are several parking garages and lots throughout the area, including the Sundance Square Garage, Houston Street Garage, and Commerce Street Garage.

If you prefer public transportation, the Trinity Railway Express (TRE) provides service from Dallas and other surrounding areas to the Fort Worth Intermodal Transportation Center, just a few blocks from Sundance Square. The Fort Worth T bus system also offers several routes that stop near Sundance Square.

If you're staying in a nearby hotel, the best option is to utilize the shuttle service. And if you're already in downtown Fort Worth, you can simply walk to Sundance Square, located in the city's heart.

GPS coordinates: 32.7530° N, 97.3291° W

Best Time to Visit: Throughout the year

Pass/Permit/Fees: General entry is free.

Did you know? It is the hub of entertainment.

4. Fort Worth Botanic Garden

The Fort Worth Botanic Garden is a 110-acre botanical garden in Fort Worth, Texas. This beautiful oasis features 23 specialty gardens, each with its unique theme and design, as well as several ponds and water features. Visitors can explore the Japanese Garden, which includes a traditional tea house and koi pond, or the Fragrance Garden, which features fragrant plants and herbs. The Fort Worth Botanic Garden also hosts several events throughout the year, including concerts, plant sales, and holiday celebrations. With its stunning displays of flora and fauna, the Fort Worth Botanic Garden is a treat to watch for nature lovers.

Location: 3220 Botanic Garden Blvd, TX, USA

Closest City or Town: Dallas, Plano.

How to Get There: On the car, the garden is just off Interstate 30, with plenty of parking available on-site. Take the University Drive exit and head north until you reach Botanic Garden Boulevard. The garden entrance will be on your right.

For public transportation, the Fort Worth T bus system offers several routes that stop near the garden, including Route 7 and Route 20. The Trinity Railway Express (TRE) also provides service from Dallas and other surrounding areas to the Fort Worth Intermodal Transportation Center, just a few miles from the garden. From there, you can take a bus or taxi to the park.

GPS coordinates: 32.7403° N, 97.3638° W

Best Time to Visit: Spring.

Pass/Permit/Fees: Tickets range from $6 to $12. Children at the age of 5 are free.

Did you know? It is a calm place. You can relax here from the hustle of life.

5. Fort Worth Water Gardens

The Fort Worth Water Gardens is a stunning downtown Fort Worth, Texas, urban park. Designed by renowned architect Philip Johnson, this unique park features several water features, including the iconic Active Pool, a 38-foot-tall central fountain surrounded by cascading terraces. Tourists can explore the tranquil Meditation Pool, a gentle treatment from the hustle and bustle of the city, or the Aerating Pool, which features a series of bubbling fountains. The Fort Worth Water Gardens is a popular destination for tourists and locals, offering a serene oasis in the city's heart.

Location: 1502 Commerce St, Fort Worth, TX 76102, USA.

Closest City or Town: North Richland Hills, TX. Watauga, TX. Benbrook, TX.

How to Get There: If you are driving, several paid parking options are nearby, including the Fort Worth Convention Center Garage and the City Place Parking Garage.

For public transportation, the T bus system offers several routes that stop near the water gardens, including Route 1, Route 2, and Route 14. The Trinity Railway Express (TRE) also provides service from Dallas and other surrounding areas to the Fort Worth Intermodal Transportation Center, just a few blocks from the gardens. You can walk toward the gardens.

GPS coordinates: 32.7477° N, 97.3266° W

Best Time to Visit: Spring, Summer.

Pass/Permit/Fees: Entry is free.

Did you know? It is famous for its beautiful, calm atmosphere and water activities.

6. Kimbell Art Museum

The Kimbell Art Museum is renowned in Fort Worth, Texas. Designed by architect Louis I. Kahn, the museum is famous for its unique blend of natural light, spatial design, and innovative architecture. The museum's permanent collection includes over 350 artworks, ranging from ancient Egyptian artifacts to contemporary masterpieces. Visitors can view results from artists such as Michelangelo, Caravaggio, Monet, and Picasso, among many others. In addition to its extensive collection, the Kimbell Art Museum hosts several temporary exhibitions throughout the year, educational programs, and special events for visitors of all ages.

Location: 3333 Camp Bowie Blvd, Fort Worth, TX 76107, USA

Closest City or Town: Plano, Irving.

How to Get There: There is ample parking available for cars on-site, nearby at the Will Rogers Memorial Center.

(TRE) provides service from Dallas and other surrounding areas to the Fort Worth Intermodal Transportation Center, a few miles from the museum. From there, you can take a bus or taxi to the museum.

If you want to walk or bike, the museum is near several popular bike and pedestrian trails, including the Trinity Trails and the Clearfork Trailhead.

GPS coordinates: 32.7486° N, 97.3649° W

Best Time to Visit: Throughout the year.

Pass/Permit/Fees: Tickets range from $14 to $18. Children at the age of 5 are free.

Did you know? It is famous worldwide for its unique architecture and collection.

7. Amon Carter Museum of American Art

The Amon Carter Museum of American Art is in Fort Worth, Texas, renowned for its extensive collection of American art, including paintings, photographs, and sculptures.

The museum's collection spans from the 19th century to contemporary art and includes works by notable American artists such as Winslow Homer, Georgia O'Keeffe, and Robert Rauschenberg. In addition to its permanent collection, the Amon Carter Museum hosts temporary exhibitions and educational programs. The museum aims to promote a deeper understanding and appreciation of American art and its role in shaping the nation's cultural heritage.

Location: 3501 Camp Bowie Blvd, Fort Worth, TX 76107, USA

Closest City or Town: Dallas, Irving.

How to Get There: You can use a GPS device or online maps to navigate to the museum's address on the car. There is ample parking available in the museum's parking lot, which is free of charge.

You can take the Trinity Metro bus route 7, which stops directly in front of the museum. Alternatively, you can take the Trinity Railway Express (TRE) to Fort Worth Central Station and then transfer to bus route 7 to get to the museum.

The nearest airport is the Dallas/Fort Worth International Airport, approximately 25 miles from the museum. To the airport, you can take a taxi, ride-sharing service, or rent a car to get to the museum.

GPS coordinates: 32.7479° N, 97.3684° W

Best Time to Visit: Throughout the year.

Pass/Permit/Fees: Entry is free.

Did you know? It is the home of American art.

8. Bass Performance Hall

Bass Performance Hall is a world-class performing arts venue in downtown Fort Worth, Texas. The hall features stunning acoustics and an exquisite European-inspired design, with a seating capacity of up to 2,056 people. It hosts performances ranging from classical music to Broadway shows and popular concerts. The hall's exterior is also impressive, featuring a 48-foot tall outdoor sculpture called "The Angels of Freedom" and a grand façade made of limestone and granite.

Bass Performance Hall is a cultural landmark in Fort Worth and a must-visit destination for anyone interested in the arts.

Location: 525 Commerce St, Fort Worth, TX 76102, USA.

Closest City or Town: Irving, Plano.

How to Get There: You can use a GPS device or online maps to navigate to the hall's address in the car—many options, including the Sundance Square Garage, Houston Street Garage, and Commerce Street Garage.

You can take the Trinity Railway Express (TRE) or the Fort Worth Transportation Authority (T) bus service to the Fort Worth Intermodal Transportation Center (ITC). You can have a short walk to the hall.

From out of town, the nearest airport is the Dallas/Fort Worth International Airport, approximately 25 miles from the hall. You can hire a taxi or ride-sharing service to the airport or rent a car to get to the entrance.

GPS coordinates: 32.7549° N, 97.3299° W

Best Time to Visit: Throughout the year.

Pass/Permit/Fees: Different prices depending upon programs.

Did you know? It is famous for its classical music programs and art.

9. Texas Motor Speedway

Texas Motor Speedway is a premier motorsports facility in Fort Worth, Texas. The track hosts several major racing events, including NASCAR Cup, IndyCar Series, and the annual Texas Truck Series race. In addition to racing events, the Speedway also hosts concerts, festivals, and other special events.

The facility features state-of-the-art amenities, including luxury suites, a high-definition video board, and a massive infield Fan Zone for fans to enjoy. Texas Motor Speedway is a must-visit destination for racing fans and a key contributor to the local economy in Fort Worth.

Location: 3545 Lone Star Cir, Fort Worth, TX 76177, United States.

Closest City or Town: Irving, Dallas.

How to Get There: You can use a GPS device or online maps to navigate to the Speedway's address if you are driving. The Speedway has multiple parking options.

The Fort Worth Intermodal Transportation Center (ITC) is the nearest train station. You can take a shuttle or bus service to the Speedway.

The nearest airport is the Dallas/Fort Worth International Airport. To the airport, you may hire a taxi, ride-sharing service, or rent a car to get to the Speedway.

Plan for traffic and parking, especially on race days and significant events.

GPS coordinates: 33.0375° N, 97.2847° W

Best Time to visit: On race day.

Pass/Permit/Fees: Tickets range from $10 to $49. Children at the age of 12 are free.

Did you know? It is famous for its race events.

10. Bureau of Engraving and Printing

The Bureau of Engraving and Printing is a federal government agency responsible for producing and distributing paper currency for the United States. The Fort Worth facility has billions of dollars' worth of U.S. currency each year, including Federal Reserve notes and other security documents. The facility offers free tours to the public, providing a unique opportunity to see the process of currency production up close.

The Bureau of Engraving and Printing plays a vital role in the economy of the United States and is an essential institution for preserving the integrity of U.S. currency.

Location: 9000 Blue Mound Rd, Fort Worth, TX 76131, United States

Closest City or Town: Irving, Dallas.

How to Get There: Website: The BEP website provides information about its services, history, and products. The website also has a contact page to submit a question or comment.

Phone: You can contact the BEP by phone at 1-844-815-8912. The phone line is available Monday through Friday from 8:00 a.m. to 3:00 p.m. Eastern Time.

Mail: You can send mail to the BEP.

In-person: The BEP has two locations to tour to see how money is made. One location is Washington, D.C., and the other is Fort Worth,

Texas. You can find more information about the tours on the BEP website.

GPS coordinates: 32.7046° N, 97.3659° W

Best Time to visit: Throughout the year

Pass/Permit/Fees: Entry is free.

Did you know? It is famous for printing currency notes.

11. Modern Art Museum of Fort Worth

The Modern Art Museum of Fort Worth is world-renowned in Fort Worth, Texas. The museum collects, presents, and interprets modern and contemporary art, focusing on works from the 1940s to the present. The building is a work of art designed by renowned Japanese architect Tadao Ando, featuring a striking combination of glass, concrete, and steel. The museum's permanent collection includes more than 3,000 works of art by artists such as Andy Warhol, Mark Rothko, and Jackson Pollock. The museum also hosts a rotating schedule of exhibitions and programs, including film screenings, lectures, and performances.

Location: 3200 Darnell St, Fort Worth, TX 76107, United States

Closest City or Town: Plano, Dallas.

How to Get There: Car: The museum is accessible by car, and a parking garage is next to the museum.

Public Transportation: The Trinity Metro bus system provides public transportation to the museum. Bus routes 2 and 7 both stop near the museum. You can use their website's Trinity Metro trip planner to plan your route.

Bike: The museum is near several bike trails, including the Trinity Trails and the Clearfork

Trail. Bike racks are outside the museum for visitors who wish to bike to the museum.

Rideshare: You can also use a ride-sharing service like Uber or Lyft to get to the museum.

GPS coordinates 32.7492° N, 97.3633° W

Best Time to visit: Throughout the year.

Pass/Permit/Fees: Tickets range from $14 to $25. Children at the age of 16 are free.

Did you know? The museum is famous for its art.

ARLINGTON

1. Six Flags Over Texas

Six Flags Over Texas is a world-famous amusement park in Arlington, Texas. Six Flags Over Texas features more than 40 thrilling rides, including roller coasters, water rides, and attractions for children. Some of the park's most popular rides include the Titan, Mr. Freeze Reverse Blast, and the New Texas Giant. The park offers live entertainment, shopping, and dining options. Six Flags Over Texas is a must-visit destination for thrill-seekers and families looking for a fun-filled day of adventure.

Location: Arlington, TX 76011, United States

Closest City or Town: Kennedale, Grand Prairie, Mansfield, and Fort Worth.

How to Get There: You can go by car, and a large parking lot is available for visitors.

The Trinity Metro bus system provides public transportation to the park. You can use their website's Trinity Metro trip planner to plan your route.

You can also book a taxi or ride to get to the park.

GPS coordinates 32.7550° N, 97.0703° W

Best Time to visit: Spring, Summer.

Pass/Permit/Fees: Different prices during on and off-season.

 Did you know? It is a worldwide famous amusement park.

2. Top O'Hill Terrace

Top O'Hill Terrace is a historic site in Arlington, Texas, USA. In the early 20th century, it was a popular destination for illegal gambling and bootlegging, attracting famous gangsters such as Bugsy Siegel and Al Capone. The site is owned by a wealthy businessman T.E. "Aunt" May, who built a luxurious casino and restaurant. During Prohibition, Top O'Hill Terrace became a hotspot for underground activities, with secret tunnels and hidden rooms used to smuggle alcohol and evade law enforcement. The site has been restored and transformed into a conference center and museum, offering a glimpse into a fascinating era of American history.

Location: 3001 W Division St, Arlington, TX 76012, USA

Closest City or Town: Dallas, Fort Worth.

How to Get There: Determine your starting location and plan your route to Arlington, Texas.

1. Once in Arlington, head towards West Division Street.

2. Turn onto Cedarland Boulevard and continue straight until you reach the entrance to Arlington Baptist University.

3. Turn right onto the university's campus and follow the signs to Top O'Hill Terrace.

4. You can park in the designated parking area and walk up the hill to the entrance.

GPS coordinates: 32.7366° N, 97.1571° W

Best Time to visit: Spring, Fall.

Pass/Permit/Fees: Entry is free.

Did you know? It has a unique history as a former illegal gambling and bootlegging operation during the Prohibition era.

WAXAHACHIE

1. The Munster Mansion in Waxahachie

The Munster Mansion is a Gothic-style house in Waxahachie, Texas, USA, modeled after the house from the 1960s television series "The Munsters." The house was built in 2001 by a Texas businessman who was a big fan of the show and wanted to recreate the iconic home. The mansion features many of the same design elements, including a grand staircase, a stained glass window, and a pet dragon named Spot. Today, the Munster Mansion is open for tours and has become a famous tourist attraction for show fans and lovers of quirky architecture.

Location: 3636 FM813, Waxahachie, TX 75165, USA

Closest City or Town: Nash, Texas; **Oak** Leaf, Texas; Red Oak, Texas.

How to Get There: Determine your starting location and plan your route to Waxahachie, Texas.

1. Once in Waxahachie, head towards North College Street.

2. Turn left onto Baylor Street, which will become North Rogers Street.

3. Turn left onto West Main Street and continue straight for about 1 mile.

4. Turn left onto North Getzendaner Street and continue straight for approximately 0.5 miles.

5. The Munster Mansion will be on your right-hand side, at the corner of North Getzendaner Street and Milam Street.

GPS coordinates 32.4356° N, 96.8108° W

Best Time to visit: Spring, Fall.

Pass/Permit/Fees: The tour ticket costs $25.

Did you know? It is famous for its unique design.

GLEN ROSE

1. Fossil Rim Wildlife Center

Fossil Rim Wildlife Center is a wildlife conservation center in Glen Rose, Texas, USA, specializing in breeding and conserving endangered species. The center spans over 1,800 acres and is home to over 1,000 animals of 50 species, including cheetahs, giraffes, rhinoceroses, and zebras. Visitors can explore the park on guided tours, observe these animals up close, and learn about their habitats, behaviors, and conservation efforts. Fossil Rim Wildlife Center is also home to a state-of-the-art veterinary hospital, where injured or sick animals are treated and rehabilitated before being released back into the wild.

Location: 2299 Co Rd 2008, Glen Rose, TX 76043, USA

Closest City or Town: Cleburne, TX Stephenville, TX · Crowley, TX · Burleson, TX .

How to Get There: Determine your starting location and route to Glen Rose, Texas.

1. Once in Glen Rose, take FM 200 north towards Somervell County Road 2008.

2. Turn left onto Somervell County Road 2008 and continue straight for about 3 miles.

3. Turn right onto Fossil Rim Road and continue straight for about 2 miles.

4. The entrance to Fossil Rim Wildlife Center will be on your left-hand side.

GPS coordinates 32.1795° N, 97.7972° W

Best Time to visit: April- May

Pass/Permit/Fees: Tickets range from $24.95 to $29.95. Children at the age of 2 are free.

Did you know? You can observe wildlife closely here.

2. Dinosaur Valley State Park:

Dinosaur Valley State Park is a 1,524-acre park in Glen Rose, Texas, USA, known for its rich history and abundant dinosaur tracks. Visitors can see some of the best-preserved dinosaur tracks in the world, including trails from theropods and sauropods, which date back over 113 million years. The park also features a range of recreational activities, such as hiking, biking, fishing, swimming, and camping, making it a popular destination for families and outdoor enthusiasts. Additionally, the park's scenic trails and stunning natural beauty make it an ideal destination for photographers and nature lovers.

Location: Glen Rose, TX 76043, USA

Closest City or Town: Cleburne, TX · Stephenville, TX · Crowley, TX · Burleson, TX.

How to Get There: Determine your starting location and route to Glen Rose, Texas.

1. Once in Glen Rose, take US-67 south towards the city center.

2. Turn right onto FM 205 and continue straight for about 4 miles.

3. Turn right onto Park Road 59 and continue straight for about 1.5 miles.

4. The entrance to Dinosaur Valley State Park will be on your left-hand side.

GPS coordinates 32.2462° N, 97.8134° W.

Best Time to visit: March-November

Pass/Permit/Fees: The ticket range is $8.

Did you know? The park is famous for Dinosaur preserves and recreational activities.

GRANBURY

1. Granbury City Beach

Granbury City Beach is a beautiful and popular recreational area on the shore of Lake Granbury in Texas, United States. The beach offers a variety of activities for visitors to enjoy, including swimming, fishing, boating, and sunbathing. The beach's lush green park features picnic areas, playgrounds, and walking trails. Visitors can enjoy the beautiful view of the lake and the surrounding hills. The beach is well-maintained and clean, making it an excellent spot for families and friends to spend quality time together. Overall, Granbury City Beach is a relaxing destination for those looking to experience Texas's natural beauty.

Location: 505 E Pearl St, Granbury, TX 76048, United States

Closest City or Town: Oak Trail Shores, DeCordova, Pecan Plantation.

How to Get There: If you drive from Dallas, take US-377 south towards Granbury. Once you reach Granbury, turn left onto Pearl Street and right onto Lambert Drive. Follow Lambert Drive until you reach the beach.

No direct public transportation is available to Granbury City Beach. However, you can take a bus or train to Granbury and then use a taxi or rideshare service to get to the beach.

By bike or on foot: If you're in Granbury, you can cycle or walk to the beach by following the bike path along Lambert Drive.

GPS coordinates 32.4418° N, 97.7813° W

Best Time to visit: May- October

Pass/Permit/Fees: General entry is free.

Did you know? The beach offers a variety of entertainment activities.

HICO

1. Minitank Battlefield

Minitank Battlefield is a miniature tank attraction in San Antonio, Texas, USA. Visitors can drive a tiny remote-controlled tank around a realistic battlefield with small buildings, obstacles, and enemy tanks to shoot at. The tanks are modeled after the famous German Tiger Tank and are easy to operate, making it an excellent experience for people of all ages. The battlefield also features a snack bar and shaded seating area, making it a great place to spend a few hours with friends and family. Minitank Battlefield is a unique and exciting attraction that offers a one-of-a-kind experience for tank enthusiasts and those looking for some fun and excitement.

Location: 3155 Private Rd 1481, Hico, TX 76457, USA

Closest City or Town: Stephenville, TX · Gatesville, TX · Cleburne, TX.

How to Get There: Driving from downtown San Antonio, take I-10 W and exit at Ralph Fair Road. Turn right onto Ralph Fair Road and then turn left onto Old Fredericksburg Road. Drive for about 1 mile, and Minitank Battlefield will be on your left.

No direct public transport is available to Minitank Battlefield. However, you can take a bus or train to downtown San Antonio and then use a taxi or rideshare service to get to the attraction.

If you're in the area, you can cycle or walk to Minitank Battlefield by following the bike paths or sidewalks along Old Fredericksburg Road.

GPS coordinates 32.0238° N, 98.0023° W

Best Time to visit: March-May

Pass/Permit/Fees: Different ticket packages are available.

Did you know? You can drive tiny remote-controlled tanks.

POTTSBORO

1. Island View Park

Pottsboro is a small town in Grayson County, Texas, USA, located near the shores of Lake Texoma. Island View Park is a popular attraction in Pottsboro, offering visitors access to the lake and a variety of outdoor recreational activities. The park features picnic areas, playgrounds, fishing piers, and a boat ramp, making it an ideal destination for families and outdoor enthusiasts. Island View Park also has several campsites and cabins available for rent, allowing visitors to extend their stay and enjoy the serene beauty of Lake Texoma.

Location: 87426 Preston Bend Rd, Pottsboro, TX 75076, United States

Closest City or Town: Denison, TX ·Sherman, TX ·Durant.

How to Get There: If you're driving from Dallas, take US-75 N towards McKinney and Exit 60B to merge onto TX-121 N towards Bonham. Continue on TX-121 N for about 35 miles, turn right onto FM 996 E. Drive for about 4 miles, and turn left onto Island View Road. Drive for about half a mile, and the park will be on your right.

No direct public transportation is available to Pottsboro Island View Park. However, you can take a Greyhound bus to Sherman, Texas, then use a taxi or rideshare service to get to the park.

If you're in the area, you can cycle or walk to Pottsboro Island View Park by following the bike paths or sidewalks along FM 996 E and Island View Road.

GPS coordinates 33.8596° N, 96.6711° W

Best Time to visit: Spring, Fall

Pass/Permit/Fees: The ticket cost is $7.

Did you know? It is a famous relaxing point from the hustle of life.

BLODGETT

1. Lake Bob Sandlin State Park:

Blodgett is a small town near Lake Bob Sandlin's northeastern Texas, USA shores. Lake Bob Sandlin State Park is a popular attraction in the area, offering visitors access to the lake and a variety of outdoor recreational activities. The park features camping areas, picnic areas, hiking and biking trails, fishing piers, and boat ramps, making it an ideal destination for families and outdoor enthusiasts. Lake Bob Sandlin State Park also hosts several events throughout the year, including nature walks, educational programs, and holiday celebrations. Blodgett and Lake Bob Sandlin State Park offer a peaceful escape from the city, with plenty of opportunities to enjoy nature and the outdoors.

Location: 341 State, Park Rd 2117, Pittsburg, TX 75686, USA

Closest City or Town: Denison, TX · Sherman, TX · Durant.

How to Get There: If driving from Dallas, take I-30 E towards Mount Pleasant. Take Exit 146 for US-271 towards Mount Pleasant, then turn right onto US-271 S. Drive for about 8 miles, then turn left onto FM 1520. Continue on FM 1520 for about 4 miles, and then turn right onto Park Road 21. Drive for about 2 miles, and you'll arrive at the park.

No direct public transport is available to Lake Bob Sandlin State Park. However, you can take a Greyhound bus to Mount Pleasant, Texas, and then use a taxi or rideshare service to get to the park.

If you're in the area, you can cycle or walk to Lake Bob Sandlin State Park by following the bike paths or sidewalks along FM 1520 and Park Road 21.

GPS coordinates 33.0606° N, 95.0983° W

Best Time to visit: Spring, Fall

Pass/Permit/Fees: The ticket cost is $5. Children at the age of 12 are free.

Did you know? It is a famous relaxing point from the hustle of life.

KARNACK

1. Caddo Lake State Park

Karnack is a small town in Harrison County, Texas, USA. It is famous because of the birthplace of the renowned TV personality and entertainer Johnny Carson. Karnack is also home to the Caddo Lake State Park, a popular tourist destination. The park boasts scenic hiking trails, fishing spots, and beautiful trip areas, making it an excellent place for outdoor enthusiasts. Tourists can enjoy various recreational activities, such as boating, kayaking, and birdwatching, while also learning about the rich history and ecology of the area. Karnack and the Caddo Lake State Park offer a beautiful blend of nature, history, and adventure.

Location: 245 Park Rd 2, Karnack, TX 75661, United States

Closest City or Town: Marshall, TX · Shreveport, LA · Bossier City .

How to Get There: To get to Caddo Lake State Park, you can use a car, as it is the most convenient mode of transportation. If you come from a nearby city or town, you can take a highway to Karnack. The closest major city is Shreveport, Louisiana, about an hour's drive away.

By air, the nearest airport is the Shreveport Regional Airport. You can book a car or hire a taxi to Karnack from there. Another option is to take a bus or a train to Marshall, which is about 20 miles away from Karnack. You can take a taxi or a rental car to reach Caddo Lake State Park.

GPS coordinates: 32.6824° N, 94.1767° W.

Best Time to visit: Spring, Fall

Pass/Permit/Fees: The ticket cost is $4. Children at the age of 12 are free.

Did you know? It is famous for its fantastic blend of history, adventure, and beauty.

AUSTIN

1. Bullock Texas State History Museum:

The Bullock Texas State History Museum is a museum in Austin, Texas, that showcases the history and culture of Texas. The museum features interactive exhibits and artifacts highlighting the significant events and people shaping the state's history. Visitors can explore the different galleries, such as the Story of Texas, where they can learn about the state's diverse cultural heritage, or the Texas Revolution and Republic gallery, where they can delve into the history of Texas' struggle for independence. The museum hosts educational programs and events, including lectures, workshops, and special exhibitions.

Location: 1800 Congress Ave., Austin, TX 78701, USA

Closest City or Town: Rollingwood, Texas West Lake Hills, Texas.

How to Get There: If you travel by car, you can use GPS or a map to navigate to the museum. There is paid parking available nearby and some street parking options.

If you use public transportation, you can get by bus or train to the museum. The nearest bus stop is on Congress Avenue, just a short walk from the museum. The Capital MetroRail also stops at the Downtown Station, about a 10-minute walk from the museum.

If you are downtown, you can easily walk to the museum.

GPS coordinates: 30.2803° N, 97.7391° W.

Best Time to Visit: Throughout the year.

Pass/Permit/Fees: Ticket costs $5- $12.

Did you know? It is famous for its cultural heritage.

2. Barton Springs Pool

It is a natural swimming pool in Zilker Park, Austin, Texas. It is fed by natural springs and maintains a year-round temperature of 68-70 degrees Fahrenheit. The pool is a popular recreational spot for locals and visitors, with swimming, sunbathing, and picnicking opportunities. The pool is also known for its diverse wildlife, including the endangered Barton Springs salamander, which can only be found in the pool's waters and the surrounding creek. Overall, Barton Springs Pool is a unique and refreshing oasis in the heart of Austin, providing a natural escape from the city's hot and humid climate.

Location: 2201 William Barton Dr, Austin, TX 78746, USA

Closest City or Town: Rollingwood, Texas West Lake Hills, Texas.

How to Get There: If you travel by car, several parking lots are available in and around Zilker Park. Some of these lots are free, while others require payment. It is recommended to arrive early on weekends or holidays, as parking can fill up quickly.

If you use public transportation, you can take a bus to Zilker Park or the Capital MetroRail, which stops at the Downtown Station. From there, you can take a short ride on a bus to reach Zilker Park.

If you are downtown, you can walk or bike to Zilker Park via the Ann and Roy Butler Hike and Bike Trail, which runs along Lady Bird Lake and provides a scenic route to the park.

GPS coordinates: 30.2641° N, 97.7713° W

Best Time to Visit: November-February.

Pass/Permit/Fees: Ticket costs $2- $9.

Did you know? It offers recreational activities in hot and humid weather.

3. Lady Bird Lake Hike-and-Bike Trail

The Lady Bird Lake Hike-and-Bike Trail is a beloved outdoor recreation area in downtown Austin, Texas. The 10-mile trail offers stunning views of the downtown skyline and access to parks, swimming areas, and picnic spots. The track is popular among runners, cyclists, walkers, and families, with plenty of space for everyone to enjoy. The trail also connects to other recreational areas, such as Zilker Park, Barton Springs Pool, and the Ann and Roy Butler Hike-and-Bike Trail. Whether looking for a scenic workout or a stroll, the Lady Bird Lake Hike-and-Bike Trail is a must-visit destination for anyone in the Austin area.

Location: 2 Robert T Martinez Jr St, Austin, TX 78702, USA

Closest City or Town: Cedar Park, TX; Round Rock, TX · Kyle, TX.

How to Get There: Several parking lots are located along the trail. The most considerable parking lot is at Auditorium Shores, near South 1st Street and Riverside Drive.

Capital Metro, Austin's public transportation system, has several bus routes that stop near the trail, including routes 1, 5, 7, and 10. You can use the Capital Metro App to plan your trip and purchase tickets.

Austin is a bike-friendly city, and several bike rental companies are downtown. You can rent a bike and easily access the trail.

Living in Downtown, you can easily walk to the trailhead. The trail is located just south of Lady Bird Lake and can be accessed from several points along the lakefront.

GPS coordinates: 30.2478° N, 97.7241° W

Best Time to Visit: Summer, Spring.

Pass/Permit/Fees: General Entry is free.

Did you know? It is a famous hike and bike track for recreational activities.

4. LBJ Presidential Library

The Lyndon Baines Johnson Presidential Library is a museum and research center on the University of Texas at Austin campus. The library houses over 45 million pages of historical documents, photographs, and recordings related to the life and presidency of President Johnson. Visitors can explore exhibits that showcase the events and issues of Johnson's presidency, including the Vietnam War, civil rights, and the Great Society. The library also hosts events, educational programs, and temporary exhibits annually. The LBJ Presidential Library is a fascinating destination for anyone interested in American history and politics.

Location: 2313 Red River St, Austin, TX 78705, USA

Closest City or Town: Marshall, TX ·Shreveport, LA · Bossier City.

How to Get There: Various transportation options are available to get to the library, including taxis, buses, and ride-sharing services like Uber or Lyft.

If you are driving, free parking is available at the library for visitors.

GPS coordinates. 30.2859° N, 97.7293° W

Best Time to visit: Throughout the year.

Pass/Permit/Fees: Ticket costs $3-$10. Children at the age of 12 are free.

Did you know? It is a knowledgeable place about American history and politics.

5. Texas State Capitol

The Texas State Capitol is a stunning example of 19th-century Renaissance Revival architecture in Austin, Texas. The capitol building is 308 feet tall, making it the sixth-tallest state capitol in the United States. The exterior is made of pink granite quarried in Marble Falls, Texas, and the interior features beautiful marble floors and grand staircases. Visitors can take free tours of the building, including the dome and legislative chambers, and learn about the history of Texas and its government. The Capitol grounds also feature monuments and statues honoring notable Texans and beautiful gardens and fountains.

Location: 1100 Congress Ave., Austin, TX 78701, USA

Closest City or Town: Marshall, TX ·Shreveport.

How to get: Various transportation options are available to get to the capitol, including taxis, buses, and ride-sharing services Uber or Lyft. If you are driving, several public parking garages nearby offer paid parking.

GPS coordinates. 30.2747° N, 97.7404° W

Best Time to visit: Throughout the year.

Pass/Permit/Fees: Entry is free.

Did you know? It is a hub to learn about Texas.

6. Zilker Metropolitan Park

Zilker Metropolitan Park is a popular public park in the heart of Austin, Texas. Spanning over 350 acres, it is one of the biggest amusement parks in the United States. The park has numerous recreational facilities, including hiking and biking trails, playgrounds, picnic areas, and a large swimming pool. It also features several iconic landmarks, such as the Zilker Botanical Garden, the Umlauf Sculpture Garden, and Barton Springs. This natural spring-fed collection maintains a temperature of 68 degrees year-round. The park is famous for outdoor events and festivals, including the annual Austin City Limits Music Festival.

Location: Austin, TX 78746, USA

Closest City or Town: Marshall, TX ·Shreveport.

How to get: Various transportation options are available to get to the park, including taxis, buses, and ride-sharing services.

If you are driving, a large parking lot is available at the park, but it can get busy on weekends and during events.

GPS coordinates. 30.2670° N, 97.7730° W

Best Time to visit: Throughout the year

Pass/Permit/Fees: Ticket range $5-$10.

Did you know? It offers a wide range of amusement activities.

7. The Driskill

The Driskill is a historic luxury hotel in downtown Austin, Texas. Built in 1886 by cattle baron Jesse Driskill, it is one of the oldest operating hotels in the state. The hotel features beautiful architecture and design, including a grand lobby with marble floors, stained glass windows, and a stunning chandelier. The guest rooms are elegantly decorated with antique furnishings and modern amenities. The Driskill offers guests several options: a fine dining restaurant, a café, and a bar. The hotel is also famous for weddings and events, with several ballrooms and meeting spaces available.

Location: 604 Brazos St, Austin, TX 78701, USA

Closest City or Town: Marshall, TX · Shreveport.

How to get: Various transportation options are available to get to the hotel, including taxis, buses, and ride-sharing services. If you are driving, valet parking is available at the hotel for a fee.

GPS coordinates. 30.2682° N, 97.7418° W

Best Time to visit: Throughout the year

Pass/Permit/Fees: Entry is free.

Did you know? It is famous for its architecture and fine dining.

8. University of Texas at Austin

The University of Texas at Austin, also known as UT Austin or simply UT, is a prestigious public research university in Austin, Texas. There are 51,000 students enrolled in undergraduate and graduate programs. UT Austin offers over 170 fields of study across 18 colleges and schools, including the highly ranked McCombs School of Business, Cockrell School of Engineering, and Moody College of Communication. The university is known for its cutting-edge energy, medicine, and technology research and renowned Longhorn athletics program.

Location: Austin, TX, United States

Closest City or Town: Jollyville, TX · Anderson Mill.

How to get: Transportation options are available to the university, including taxis, buses, and ride-sharing services. If you are driving, several parking garages and lots are available on campus, but they can get busy during peak times.

GPS coordinates. 30.2849° N, 97.7341° W

Best Time to visit: Throughout the year.

Pass/Permit/Fees: Entry is free.

Did you know? It is a prestigious institute and worldwide famous for research and education.

9. Museum of the Weird

The Museum of the Weird is a unique and quirky attraction in downtown Austin, Texas. It features a collection of oddities, curiosities, and artifacts that range from the bizarre to the downright creepy. Some popular exhibits include shrunken heads, two-headed animals, a mummified mermaid, and a vampire killing kit. Visitors can also see live performances of magic shows, sideshow acts, and sword swallowing. The museum offers a fun and immersive experience that will leave a lasting impression on visitors looking for something out of the ordinary.

Location: 412 E 6th St, Austin, TX 78701, USA

Closest City or Town: Jollyville, TX · Anderson Mill.

How to get: The museum is in downtown Austin, near the famous Sixth Street entertainment district. Transportation options are available at the museum, including taxis, buses, and ride-sharing services. If you are driving, street parking is available nearby but can be limited and expensive during peak times.

GPS coordinates. 30.2672° N, 97.7387° W

Best Time to visit: Throughout the year

Pass/Permit/Fees: Ticket costs $12

Did you know? It is a famous place for magic shows.

BURNET

1. Longhorn Cavern State Park

Longhorn Cavern State Park is a unique and fascinating attraction in Burnet County, Texas. It is home to underground limestone caves formed over millions of years by water flow. Visitors can take guided tours through the caverns, filled with stunning rock formations, underground lakes, and interesting geological features. The park has many hiking trails, picnic areas, and a visitor center with exhibits on the history and geology of the site. Longhorn Cavern State Park is a must-visit place for nature lovers.

Location: 6211 Park Road 4 S, Burnet, TX 78611, USA

Closest City or Town: Lampasas, Bell, Williamson, Travis, Blanco, Llano.

How to get: The Park is located in Burnet County, about 1.5 hours northwest of Austin. Various transportation options are available at the park, including driving, taxi, or ride-sharing services. If you are going, there is ample parking available on-site.

GPS coordinates. 30.6839° N, 98.3523° W

Best Time to Visit: Throughout the year

Pass/Permit/Fees: Entry is free

Did you know? It is home to ancient underground limestone caves.

2. Inks Lake State Park:

Inks Lake State Park is a beautiful and popular destination in Burnet County, Texas. It is situated on Inks Lake's banks, a picturesque water body that offers opportunities for swimming, fishing, boating, and other water activities. The park also features miles of hiking trails, picnic areas, and campsites for overnight stays. Visitors can enjoy scenic views of the surrounding hill country, as well as a variety of wildlife and plant species. Inks Lake State Park is a perfect place for families to relax.

Location: 3630 Park Rd 4 W, Burnet, TX 78611, USA

Closest City or Town: Lampasas, Bell, Williamson, Travis, Blanco, Llano.

How to get: The park is located in Burnet County, about 1.5 hours northwest of Austin. Various transportation options are available at the park, including driving, taxi, or ride-sharing services. If you are going, there is ample parking available on-site.

GPS coordinates. 30.7374° N, 98.3690° W

Best Time to Visit: Throughout the year.

Pass/Permit/Fees: The ticket costs $7. Kids under 13 are free.

Did you know? It is a house of water activities—the perfect place for families.

GEORGETOWN

1. Inner Space Cavern

Inner Space Cavern is a fascinating geological wonder in Georgetown, Texas, United States. It was discovered in 1963 by a Texas Highway Department drilling team and was opened to the public in 1966. The cave system is around 10,000 years old and stretches over 2.5 miles.

Visitors can take guided cavern tours and witness incredible natural formations such as stalactites, stalagmites, flowstones, and columns. The temperature inside the cave is a cool 72°F (22°C), making it a pleasant place to explore during the hot Texas summers.

In addition to the regular tours, Inner Space Cavern offers specialty tours for those interested in photography, spelunking, or more in-depth geological information.

Location: 4200 S I-35 Frontage Rd, Georgetown, TX 78626, USA

Closest City or Town: Leander, TX · Cedar Park, TX.

How to get: If you drive from Austin, take I-35 North towards Georgetown and exit 259. Stay on the I-35 Frontage Road for about 1 mile, and you will see the entrance to Inner Space Cavern on your right-hand side.

GPS coordinates. 30.5254° N, 97.7148° W.

Best Time to Visit: Summer

Pass/Permit/Fees: Ticket costs $15.95-$ 21.95. Kids under 4 are free.

Did you know? It's a unique destination for nature enthusiasts, families, and those interested in learning more about the world's natural wonders.

BEND

1. Gorman Falls

Enjoy the natural splendor of Gorman Falls, a hidden gem in Colorado Bend State Park, Texas. Feel the thrill of the 65-foot waterfall crashing into a fern-covered grotto. The trek to the falls is difficult, but the beautiful vista is well worth the effort. Other activities at the park include fishing, swimming, and camping under the Texas sky.

Location: Colorado Bend State Park, Bend, TX 76824

Closest City or Town: Lampasas, Texas (nearby)

How to get: From Lampasas, take US-281 N. Turn right onto FM 580 W. Drive to Colorado Bend State Park Rd.

GPS coordinates. 31.0582° N, 98.4823° W

Best Time to Visit: The park is open year-round but late spring to early summer is the best time to visit when the falls are at their fullest.

Pass/Permit/Fees: Entry fee is $5 for adults, children under 12 are free.

Did you know? Gorman Falls is a "living" waterfall - it continues to grow and change due to the high amount of calcium in the water.

SPICEWOOD

1. Krause Springs

Spicewood is a small Texas Hill Country town known for its beautiful natural surroundings and laid-back lifestyle. One of its most popular attractions is Krause Springs, a privately owned swimming hole and camping area with natural spring-fed pools, waterfalls, and towering cypress trees. Visitors can swim, sunbathe, or picnic on the grounds, offering hiking trails, campsites, and RV hookups. In addition to Krause Springs, Spicewood is home to several wineries, distilleries, restaurants, and the Pedernales River, which offers kayaking, fishing, and other water-based activities.

Location: 424 Co Rd 404, Spicewood, TX 78669, USA

Closest City or Town: Lakeway, TX · Leander, TX.

How to get: From Austin, take TX-71 west toward Spicewood.

Turn left onto Paleface Ranch Road, just past the Pedernales River.

Follow Paleface Ranch Road for about 2 miles, then turn left onto County Road 404.

After about 1 mile, turn right onto County Road 403.

Follow County Road 403 for about half a mile until you see the entrance to Krause Springs on your left.

Once you arrive at Krause Springs, pay the admission fee at the gate and park your vehicle in the designated area.

From there, you can explore the swimming hole, waterfalls, and other natural features or set up camp if you're staying overnight.

GPS coordinates. 30.4777° N, 98.1517° W

Best Time to Visit: Summer, Spring

Pass/Permit/Fees: The ticket range is $5-$8. Kids under 4 are free.

Did you know? It offers multiple amusement activities.

Willow City

1. Willow City Loop

It is a scenic drive in the Texas Hill Country, known for its stunning displays of wildflowers and picturesque landscapes. The 13-mile route takes visitors through rolling hills, pastures, and rugged canyons, providing hiking, photography, and wildlife-watching opportunities. In the spring, the area explodes with vibrant displays of bluebonnets, Indian paintbrushes, and other wildflowers, drawing visitors from all over the state. The loop is also home to several historic sites, ranches, and numerous camping and picnic areas.

Location: Willow City Loop Fredericksburg, TX 78624

Closest City or Town: Llano, Johnson City.

How to get: From Fredericksburg, Texas, head north on Highway 16.

After about 13 miles, turn right onto Willow City Loop Road.

Follow Willow City Loop Road for the 13-mile route, which winds through rolling hills, pastures, and rugged canyons.

Along the way, you'll have plenty of opportunities to stop and enjoy the stunning scenery, including wildflowers, historic sites, and ranches.

Once you reach the end of the loop, turn around and follow your steps back to Fredericksburg.

GPS coordinates. 30.3104° N, 98.6824° W

Best Time to Visit: Summer, Spring

Pass/Permit/Fees: Entry is free.

Did you know? It looks stunning natural beauty, particularly during the spring when wildflowers bloom.

FREDERICKSBURG

1. Grape Creek Vineyards Fredericksburg

Grape Creek Vineyards is a winery in Fredericksburg, Texas, that produces various award-winning wines from estate-grown grapes. The winery features a tasting room where visitors can sample a selection of wines and learn about the winemaking process and a beautifully landscaped courtyard where guests can relax and enjoy the scenic views. Grape Creek Vineyards also offers tours of the vineyard, winery, and many events and activities throughout the year, including wine and food pairings, live music, and grape stomps. Overall, Grape Creek Vineyards is a must-visit destination for wine lovers visiting Fredericksburg.

Location: 10587 US-290, Fredericksburg, TX 78624, USA

Closest City or Town: Blowout, TX. Doss, TX.

How to get: Take US Highway 290 east from Fredericksburg for about 9 miles.

Turn left onto Grape Creek Road (at the intersection with FM 1826).

Follow Grape Creek Road for approximately 1.5 miles.

You will see the entrance to Grape Creek Vineyards on your left.

Turn left into the opening and follow the road to the parking area.

GPS coordinates. 30.2214° N, 98.7203° W

Best Time to Visit: Summer, Spring

Pass/Permit/Fees: The ticket costs $155.

Did you know? It is a perfect place for wine lovers.

2. National Museum of the Pacific War

The National Museum of the Pacific War is in Fredericksburg, Texas. It preserves the memory and history of the Pacific War during World War II. The museum houses a vast collection of artifacts, exhibits, and interactive displays that provide visitors with a comprehensive and immersive experience of the war in the Pacific. The museum also includes a research center, a library, and a memorial courtyard honoring those who served in the Pacific War. The museum hosts various events and educational programs throughout the year.

Location: 311 E Austin St, Fredericksburg, TX 78624, USA

Closest City or Town: Blowout, TX. Doss, TX.

How to get: Take Main Street (Highway 290) from Fredericksburg east towards the historic district.

Turn left onto Adams Street (at the intersection with Llano Street).

Continue on Adams Street for one block, then turn right onto Austin Street.

The National Museum of the Pacific War will be on your right, at the intersection of Austin Street and East Austin Street.

GPS coordinates. 30.2733° N, 98.8679° W

Best Time to Visit: Throughout the year

Pass/Permit/Fees: The tickets range from $10-$24. Kids under 6 are free.

Did you know? It is the home of the collection of the Pacific War.

3. Main Street

Main Street Fredericksburg is the heart of the historic district in Fredericksburg, Texas. This charming thoroughfare is known for its well-preserved 19th-century buildings, which now house various unique shops, restaurants, and galleries. Main Street is also home to the iconic Vereins Kirche, a replica of the original German church that served as a community center for early settlers. Visitors can stroll along the street, taking in the picturesque storefronts and quaint ambiance, or attend one of the many annual events here, such as the Fredericksburg Food and Wine Fest or Oktoberfest.

Location: 100 block of East Main Street, Fredericksburg, TX 78624

Closest City or Town: Blowout, TX. Doss, TX.

How to get: Main Street Fredericksburg is located in the historic district of Fredericksburg, Texas, and can be accessed from Highway 290.

GPS coordinates. 30.2753° N, 98.8718° W

Best Time to Visit: Throughout the year

Pass/Permit/Fees: Free Entry

Did you know? It is a vibrant place to hang out.

4. Wildseed Farms

Wildseed Farms is a sprawling wildflower farm and event venue in Fredericksburg, Texas. The farm spans over 200 acres and boasts over 70 species of wildflowers, making it the largest working wildflower farm in the country. Visitors can wander through fields of colorful blooms, pick up seeds and plants at the farm store, or enjoy a meal at the on-site cafe. Wildseed Farms also hosts various events throughout the year, including concerts, wine tastings, and the annual Butterfly and Native Plant Festival. A visit to Wildseed Farms is a must-see attraction for anyone visiting the Texas Hill Country.

Location: 100 Legacy Dr, Fredericksburg, TX 78624, USA

Closest City or Town: Doss, TX.

How to get: It can be accessed via Highway 290.

GPS coordinates. 30.2223° N, 98.7679° W

Best Time to Visit: Spring

Pass/Permit/Fees: Free Entry

Did you know? It is the home of joy & fun.

5. Enchanted Rock State Natural Are

Enchanted Rock State Natural Area is a popular park located in the Texas Hill Country, approximately 18 miles north of Fredericksburg. The park's centerpiece is Enchanted Rock, a large pink granite dome that rises 425 feet. Visitors can hike to Rock for stunning views or explore the park's many hiking trails, picnic areas, and campsites. The park is also known for its stargazing opportunities, as it is located far from any major cities and has minimal light pollution. Enchanted Rock State Natural Area is a destination for nature lovers and outdoor enthusiasts.

Location: 16710 Ranch Rd 965, Fredericksburg, TX 78624, USA

Closest City or Town: Blowout, TX.

How to get: Visitors can reach the park via Ranch Road.

GPS coordinates. 30.4951° N, 98.8200° W

Best Time to Visit: Spring, Summer.

Pass/Permit/Fees: The ticket costs $8. Kids under 12 are free.

Did you know? It is a must-visit place for nature lovers.

6. Rockbox Theater

Rockbox Theater is a state-of-the-art live music and entertainment venue in downtown Fredericksburg, Texas. The theater features a 392-seat auditorium and hosts many live performances, including music concerts, comedy shows, and theatrical productions. The venue has a nostalgic vibe, with its vintage decor and retro neon signage, and its intimate setting allows for an up-close and personal experience with the performers. Live shows, Rockbox Theater also offers dinner theater experiences, where guests can enjoy a meal while being entertained by the show. Rockbox Theater is a must-visit destination for anyone looking for an entertaining night in Fredericksburg.

Location: 109 Llano St, Fredericksburg, TX 78624, USA

Closest City or Town: Blowout, TX.

How to get: It is accessed by car or on foot from Main Street.

GPS coordinates. 30.2745° N, 98.8698° W

Best Time to Visit: Throughout the year.

Pass/Permit/Fees: The ticket costs $38-$52.

Did you know? It is the home of live shows and performances.

7. Pioneer Museum

The Pioneer Museum is a historical museum located in downtown Fredericksburg, Texas. The museum consists of a collection of historic structures, including a schoolhouse, a log cabin, and a Sunday house, that have been preserved and restored to showcase life in the Texas Hill Country in the 19th century. Visitors can explore the buildings and exhibits to learn about the region's early settlers, including German immigrants and Native Americans. The museum offers special events throughout the year, such as living history reenactments and holiday celebrations. The Pioneer Museum is a fascinating and educational attraction for all ages.

Location: 325 W Main St, Fredericksburg, TX 78624, USA

Closest City or Town: Blowout, TX.

How to get: It is accessed by car or on foot from Main Street.

GPS coordinates. 30.2784° N, 98.8775° W

Best Time to Visit: Throughout the year.

Pass/Permit/Fees: The ticket costs $5-$10. Kids under 6 are free.

Did you know? It is the home of historical collections.

8. Old Tunnel State Park

Old Tunnel State Park is a natural park in Fredericksburg, Texas, known for its unique wildlife and historic railroad tunnel. The tunnel is home to millions of Mexican free-tailed bats that roost from May through October, making for a spectacular nightly show for visitors. The park offers several activities like hiking trails, picnic areas, and a visitor center with information about the park's history and ecology. Old Tunnel State Park is a must-visit attraction for nature and wildlife enthusiasts visiting the Texas Hill Country.

Location: 325 W Main St, Fredericksburg, TX 78624, USA

Closest City or Town: Blowout, TX.

How to get: Visitors can access the park by car via Old San Antonio Road or by taking Exit 540 off of Interstate 10 and following the signs to the park.

GPS coordinates. 30.1012° N, 98.8208° W

Best Time to Visit: May- October

Pass/Permit/Fees: Free Entry.

Did you know? It is a must-visit place for nature and wildlife lovers.

JOHNSON CITY

1. Pedernales Falls State Park

Pedernales Falls State Park is a beautiful natural area in the Texas Hill Country, just outside Austin. The park covers over 5,000 acres and features stunning limestone cliffs, scenic hiking trails, and the Pedernales River. Visitors can do multiple activities like swimming, fishing, kayaking in the river, or exploring the park's many trails on foot or by bike. One of the park's main attractions is the Pedernales Falls, a cascading waterfall that creates a breathtaking natural landscape. The park also offers camping facilities, picnic areas, and educational programs.

Location: 2585 Park Rd 6026, Johnson City, TX 78636, USA

Closest City or Town: Fredericksburg, TX · Canyon Lake.

How to get: To get there, you can take Highway 290 West towards Johnson City and follow the signs to the park.

GPS coordinates. 30.3081° N, 98.2577° W

Best Time to Visit: Summer, Spring

Pass/Permit/Fees: The ticket costs $6. Kids under 13 are free.

Did you know? It is an ideal place to connect with nature.

2. Lyndon B Johnson National Historical Park

Lyndon B Johnson National Historical Park is a 1,570-acre site in the Texas Hill Country that is preserving and promoting the legacy of President Lyndon B. Johnson. The park is in Stonewall, Texas, and includes several historic sites, such as the Johnson family ranch, the Texas White House, and the President's boyhood home. Visitors can take guided tours of these sites, watch films about Johnson's life and presidency, and explore exhibits highlighting the accomplishments and challenges of his time in office.

Location: 1048 Park Road #49, Stonewall, TX 78671, USA

Closest City or Town: Fredericksburg, TX · Canyon Lake.

How to get: Lyndon B Johnson National Historical Park is in Stonewall, Texas, about an hour's drive west of Austin and two hours north of San Antonio. To get there, you can take US Highway 290 to Stonewall and follow the signs to the park.

GPS coordinates. 30.2425° N, 98.6085° W

Best Time to Visit: Throughout the year.

Pass/Permit/Fees: Free Entry.

Did you know? It offers hiking trails, picnic areas, and educational programs on the history of the US.

DRIPPING SPRINGS

1. Hamilton Pool Preserve

Hamilton Pool Preserve is a natural place for swimming in Dripping Springs, Texas. It existed when an underground river's dome collapsed. The pool is surrounded by limestone cliffs and fed by a 50-foot waterfall, creating a stunning oasis in the middle of the Texas Hill Country. The preserve is also home to various plant and animal species, including the Golden-cheeked Warbler and the Black-capped Vireo, both endangered species. Visitors can swim in the calm, turquoise waters or hike through the nature preserve, which features trails through oak and juniper trees and along the creek bed.

Location: 24300 Hamilton Pool Rd, Dripping Springs, TX, US

Closest City or Town: Lakeway, TX · Kyle, TX.

How to get: You can follow Ranch Road 12 to Hamilton Pool Road.

GPS coordinates. 30.3423° N, 98.1271° W

Best Time to Visit: Spring, Fall

Pass/Permit/Fees: Reservation will be online.

Did you know? It is a perfect place for water activities.

WIMBERLEY

1. Jacob's Well

Jacob's Well is a natural spring in Wimberley, Texas, approximately 30 miles southwest of Austin. It is one of the vast underwater caves in Texas, with a diameter of about 12 feet and a depth of 140 feet. The water is crystal clear and remains a constant 68 degrees Fahrenheit year-round. The well feeds Cypress Creek, which flows through the Texas Hill Country and eventually into the Blanco River. Jacob's Well is a popular destination for swimming, diving, and exploring the region's natural beauty. However, due to its depth and strong currents, it is recommended for experienced swimmers and divers only.

Location: 221 Woodacre Drive, Wimberley, TX

Closest City or Town: Lakeway, TX · Kyle, TX.

How to get: You can take Ranch Road 12 south for about 3 miles, then turn left onto Mount Sharp Road and continue for approximately 1.5 miles.

GPS coordinates. 30.0344° N, 98.1261° W

Best Time to Visit: Spring, Fall

Pass/Permit/Fees: Free Entry.

Did you know? It is a perfect place to explore nature.

2. Blue Hole Regional Park

Blue Hole Regional Park is a natural park in Wimberley, Texas, approximately 30 miles southwest of Austin. The park spans over 126 acres and features a raw swimming hole, hiking and biking trails, a playscape, picnic areas, and a pavilion. The nearby Cypress Creek feeds the clear blue-green water of the swimming hole and remains a constant 72 degrees Fahrenheit year-round. The park has camping facilities, including RV sites and tent camping areas.

Location: 100 Blue Hole Ln, Wimberley, TX 78676, USA

Closest City or Town: Lakeway, TX · Kyle, TX.

How to get: Take Ranch Road 12 south for about 2.5 miles, then turn right onto Blue Hole Lane and continue for about half a mile until you reach the park entrance.

GPS coordinates. 30.0010° N, 98.0907° W

Best Time to Visit: Spring, Summer.

Pass/Permit/Fees: The ticket costs $6-$12. Kids under 3 are free.

Did you know? It is a famous place for outdoor activities.

COLLEGE STATION

1. George Bush Presidential Library and Museum

It is on the campus of Texas A&M University. The museum shows the life and legacy of President George H.W. Bush and includes exhibits on his time in office, his family, and his role in international events. The museum presents a replica of the Oval Office, a section dedicated to the first lady, Barbara Bush, and a collection of presidential gifts and artifacts. Additionally, the library holds a vast array of documents and records related to President Bush's presidency and the policies of his administration, which are available to researchers and the public.

Location: 1000 George Bush Dr. W, College Station, TX 77845, USA

Closest City or Town: Bryan, TX.

How to get: Take the University Drive exit from Texas Highway 6 and head east, then turn right onto George Bush Drive West and continue for about half a mile until you reach the museum.

GPS coordinates. 30.5965° N, 96.3533° W

Best Time to Visit: Throughout the year.

Pass/Permit/Fees: The ticket costs $3-$9.

Did you know? It is the best place to learn about George H.W. Bush.

SAN ANTONIO

1. San Fernando De Bexar Cathedral

The San Fernando De Bexar Cathedral is a historic Catholic church in San Antonio, Texas. The church is rich in history and has been a cornerstone of the community for centuries. It played a significant role in the Texas Revolution. The cathedral's stunning architecture features Gothic-style spires and intricate stonework, making it a popular destination for tourists and history enthusiasts. Today, the San Fernando De Bexar Cathedral is a sign of worship and a symbol of San Antonio's rich cultural heritage.

Location: 115 Main Plaza, San Antonio, TX 78205, USA

Closest City or Town: Kirby, TX.

How to get: The San Fernando De Bexar Cathedral is located in downtown San Antonio, Texas, and can be accessed by car, public transportation, or on foot.

GPS coordinates. 29.4245° N, 98.4940° W

Best Time to Visit: Throughout the year.

Pass/Permit/Fees: Free Entry.

Did you know? It is famous for its heritage and worship.

2. San Antonio Missions National Historical Park

It has a cultural and historical landmark in San Antonio, Texas. The park includes five Spanish colonial missions established in the 18th century by Franciscan missionaries to convert Native Americans to Christianity. The missions, which include the Alamo, were announced as a UNESCO World Heritage Site and mentioned as one of Spanish colonial architecture in the United States. Visitors can explore the missions' churches, living quarters, and agricultural fields.

Location: San Antonio, TX 78214, United States

Closest City or Town: Converse, TX.

How to get: It is located in San Antonio, Texas, and can be accessed by car or public transportation.

GPS coordinates. 29.3293° N, 98.4536° W

Best Time to Visit: Throughout the year.

Pass/Permit/Fees: Free Entry.

Did you know? It is famous for its historical and cultural landmarks.

3. Japanese Tea Gardens

The Japanese Tea Gardens, also known as the Sunken Gardens, is a serene park in San Antonio, Texas. Originally built as a quarry in the early 20th century, the gardens were transformed into a Japanese-inspired oasis in the 1920s. Visitors can stroll through the lush gardens, which feature koi ponds, waterfalls, and a tea house. The park also includes a Japanese-style pagoda and a 60-foot waterfall, a popular photography spot. The Japanese Tea Garden is famous for offering a peaceful escape from the hustle and bustle of the city.

Location: 3220 Botanic Garden Blvd, Fort Worth, TX 76107, United States

Closest City or Town: Schertz, TX .

How to get: The Japanese Tea Gardens are located in Brackenridge Park, San Antonio, Texas, and can be accessed by car, public transportation, or on foot.

GPS coordinates. 32.7355° N, 97.3663° W

Best Time to Visit: Spring.

Pass/Permit/Fees: The ticket costs $9-$13. Kids under 6 are free.

Did you know? It is home to natural beauty.

4. Mission San Jose

Mission San Jose is a historic Catholic mission in San Antonio, Texas. The mission was part of a network of Spanish colonial missions to convert Native Americans to Christianity and expand Spain's influence in the region. The mission's stunning architecture features intricate stonework and baroque-style carvings, making it one of the most beautiful examples of Spanish colonial architecture in the United States. The mission serves as a popular tourist attraction and cultural landmark, offering visitors a glimpse into the daily life of the people who lived and worked there centuries ago.

Location: 701 E Pyron Ave, San Antonio, TX 78214, USA

Closest City or Town: Converse, TX.

How to get: It can access by car or public transportation. It is situated just off the San Antonio Missions Trail, which connects all five missions and is a popular stop for visitors exploring the trail.

GPS coordinates. 29.3622° N, 98.4788° W

Best Time to Visit: Throughout the year.

Pass/Permit/Fees: Free Entry.

Did you know? It is famous for its historical architecture.

5. Natural Bridge Caverns

Natural Bridge Caverns is a popular tourist attraction. The caverns are home to an extensive network of underground caves and formations, including stalactites, stalagmites, and underground lakes. Visitors can explore the caverns on guided tours, which show you from easy walks to more challenging spelunking adventures. The site also features an aerial adventure course, zip lines, and a maze, making it a fun destination for the whole family. Natural Bridge Caverns is committed to conservation and education, with ongoing efforts to protect the cave ecosystem and educate visitors about its importance.

Location: 26495 Natural Bridge Caverns Rd, San Antonio, TX 78266, USA

Closest City or Town: Converse, TX.

How to get: Approximately 30 minutes north of San Antonio, and can be accessed by car or shuttle bus from the on-site visitor center.

GPS coordinates. 29.6924° N, 98.3427° W

Best Time to Visit: December-February.

Pass/Permit/Fees: The ticket costs $30-$41. Kids under 3 are free.

Did you know? It is a natural wonder.

6. The Alamo

The Alamo is a historic mission and fortress in downtown San Antonio, Texas. It played a pivotal role in the Texas Revolution, as it was the site of a famous battle between Texan defenders and Mexican forces in 1836. The battle lasted for 13 days and ended in the deaths of all Texan defenders, but it became a rallying cry for Texan independence and a symbol of courage and sacrifice. The Alamo is a popular tourist attraction.

Location: 300 Alamo Plaza, San Antonio, TX 78205, USA

Closest City or Town: Leon Valley

How to get: It can be accessed by car, public transportation, or on foot.

GPS coordinates. 29.4260° N, 98.4861° W

Best Time to Visit: March-April.

Pass/Permit/Fees: Free Entry.

Did you know? It is the symbol of independence.

7. San Antonio River Walk

It is a vibrant and scenic network of walkways and bridges in downtown San Antonio, Texas. Lined with shops, restaurants, and historic landmarks, the River Walk is a popular destination for tourists and locals. Visitors can stroll along the river, take a boat tour, or enjoy a meal or a drink at one of the many riverside establishments. With its lively atmosphere and stunning views, the San Antonio River Walk is a must-see destination for anyone visiting the city.

Location: San Antonio, TX 78205, US

Closest City or Town: Leon Valley.

How to get: You can go on foot or take a river taxi or boat tour from one of the many entry points along the river.

GPS coordinates. 29.4230° N, 98.4860° W

Best Time to Visit: Throughout the year.

Pass/Permit/Fees: Free Entry.

Did you know? It is home to festivals and events.

8. McNay Art Museum

The McNay Art Museum is renowned in San Antonio, Texas. It was founded in 1954 by Marion Koogler McNay, who donated her extensive art collection and her home to establish the museum. The museum's collection features over 20,000 works of art, including paintings, sculptures, and decorative arts, from a wide range of periods and cultures. The museum hosts a variety of exhibitions and several educational programs and events for visitors. With its stunning architecture, beautiful grounds, and impressive collection, the McNay Art Museum is a must-see destination for art lovers.

Location: 6000 N New Braunfels Ave, San Antonio, TX 78209, USA

Closest City or Town: Universal City.

How to get: The McNay Art Museum is located in the Alamo Heights neighborhood of San Antonio, Texas, and can be easily accessed by car, public transportation, or on foot.

GPS coordinates. 29.4857° N, 98.4571° W

Best Time to Visit: Throughout the year.

Pass/Permit/Fees: Free Entry twice a week.

Did you know? It is home to exhibitions.

9. Majestic & Empire Theatres

The Majestic and Empire Theatres are two historic theaters in San Antonio, Texas, USA. It was built in 1929 and is a beautiful example of atmospheric theater design, with a ceiling painted to resemble a starry sky. The Empire Theatre was built in 1913 and has a Spanish Colonial Revival style. Both theaters have been beautifully restored and are now used for various performances, including concerts, plays, and dance productions. They are considered cultural landmarks of San Antonio and enchant visitors from all over the world.

Location: 224 E Houston St, San Antonio, TX 78205, USA

Closest City or Town: Live Oak.

How to get: VIA Metropolitan Transit offers several bus routes that stop near theaters. The closest bus stops are on Houston Street and St. Mary's Street.

GPS coordinates. 29.4262° N, 98.4906° W

Best Time to Visit: Throughout the year

Pass/Permit/Fees: The ticket costs $25-$150.

Did you know? It is famous for its architecture and historical culture.

10. San Antonio Botanical Garden

It is a 38-acre oasis in San Antonio, Texas, USA. It features a variety of themed gardens, including a rose garden, an herb garden, a Japanese garden, a butterfly exhibit, and a bird-watching area. The park also hosts events and educational programs throughout the year, including classes, workshops, and summer camps for children. One of the highlights of the San Antonio Botanical Garden is its Texas Native Trail, which showcases the diverse flora and fauna of the region. With its beautiful landscaping, diverse plant life, and engaging programming, the San Antonio Botanical Garden is a must-visit destination for nature lovers of all ages.

Location: 555 Funston Pl, San Antonio, TX 78209, USA

Closest City or Town: Universal City.

How to get: There is a parking lot near the garden entrance. There is also street parking available in the surrounding area.

VIA Metropolitan Transit has several bus routes that stop near the garden. The closest bus stop is on North St. Mary's Street.

GPS coordinates. 29.4577° N, 98.4574° W

Best Time to Visit: Throughout the year

Pass/Permit/Fees: The ticket costs $13-$15. Kids under 3 are free.

Did you know? It is famous for its attractive landscapes &activities.

11. San Antonio Museum of Art

The San Antonio Museum of Art is downtown San Antonio, Texas, USA. It is a house of a historic building once the Lone Star Brewery. It features a vast collection of art from around the world, focusing on ancient Mediterranean and Latin American art. The museum also hosts temporary exhibitions, educational programs, and events throughout the year, including lectures, workshops, and performances. The museum's collection includes more than 30,000 works of art, including paintings, sculptures, textiles, and decorative arts. With its diverse collection and engaging programming, the San Antonio Museum of Art is a must-visit destination for art enthusiasts of all ages.

Location: 200 W Jones Ave, San Antonio, TX 78215, USA

Closest City or Town: Schertz, TX.

How to get: A parking garage is adjacent to the museum, with accessible entry points on Avenue B and Lexington Avenue. VIA Metropolitan Transit's closest bus stop is on North St. Mary's Street and East Jones Avenue.

GPS coordinates. 29.4373° N, 98.4822° W

Best Time to Visit: Throughout the year.

Pass/Permit/Fees: The ticket costs $12-$20.

Did you know? It is famous for the world's art.

12. King William Historic District

It is in the south of downtown San Antonio, Texas, USA. It is home to an array of historic homes, buildings, and churches that date back to the 19th and early 20th centuries. The neighborhood is named after King Wilhelm I of Prussia and features a variety of architectural styles, including Victorian, Greek Revival, and Italianate. The King William Historic District is also home to various restaurants, cafes, shops, and several museums and cultural institutions, such as the Villa Finale Museum & Gardens and the Guenther House.

Location: San Antonio, TX, USA

Closest City or Town: Cesar Chavez Boulevard.

How to get: By car, you can enter the neighborhood via South Alamo Street, South St. Mary's Street, or South Presa Street. Metropolitan Transit has several bus routes near King William Historic District.

GPS coordinates. 29.4154° N, 98.4856° W.

Best Time to Visit: Throughout the year.

Pass/Permit/Fees: Free Entry.

Did you know? It is famous for its rich culture and beautiful architecture.

13. Alamo Plaza

Alamo Plaza is a historic district in the heart of downtown San Antonio, Texas, USA. It is home to the Alamo, a UNESCO World Heritage Site and one of the most famous landmarks in Texas. The plaza has a variety of historic buildings, museums, shops, and restaurants and is a popular destination for tourists and locals alike. In addition to the Alamo, other notable attractions in the area include the San Antonio River Walk, the Spanish Governor's Palace, and the Buckhorn Saloon & Museum. With its rich history and vibrant atmosphere, Alamo Plaza is a must-visit destination for anyone interested in San Antonio's heritage.

Location: San Antonio, TX 78205, USA

Closest City or Town: Bonham.

How to get: You can enter the downtown by car via Interstate 35, Interstate 10, or US Highway 281.

Metropolitan Transit has several bus routes that stop near the plaza.

GPS coordinates. 29.4256° N, 98.4860° W.

Best Time to Visit: Throughout the year

Pass/Permit/Fees: The ticket costs $5-$12.

Did you know? It is a perfect place to visit the historic buildings & museums.

14. Briscoe Western Art Museum

The Briscoe Western Art Museum is a prominent museum that preserves and showcases the art, history, and culture of the American West. The museum was founded in 2013 by the late Texas Governor Dolph Briscoe and his wife, Janey Slaughter Briscoe, avid Western art and artifacts collectors. The museum's permanent collection includes over 700 works of art and artifacts, ranging from paintings and sculptures to firearms and saddles, all of which highlight the diversity and complexity of the American West. The Briscoe Western Art Museum also hosts temporary exhibitions and educational programs for visitors of all ages.

Location: 210 W Market St, San Antonio, TX 78205, USA

Closest City or Town: Universal City.

How to get: You can reach the museum by car and park nearby.

Metropolitan Transit operates several bus routes that stop near the museum. You can also take a VIA streetcar to the museum. You can rent a bike or scooter from one of the many rental companies in downtown San Antonio and ride to the museum.

GPS coordinates. 29.4230° N, 98.4891° W

Best Time to Visit: Throughout the year.

Pass/Permit/Fees: The ticket costs $8-$14. Kids under 12 are free.

Did you know? It has a vast collection of art.

15. The DoSeum - San Antonio's Museum for Kids

The DoSeum is a world-class children's museum in San Antonio, Texas that offers a variety of interactive exhibits and educational programs designed to inspire and engage children of all ages. The museum aims to provide a stimulating environment for children to learn and grow through play, exploration, and creativity. The DoSeum features a range of exhibits and activities, including a sensory garden, a bubble exhibit, a spy academy, and a musical staircase. It also offers workshops, classes, and camps for children and families throughout the year.

Location: 2800 Broadway, San Antonio, TX 78209, US

Closest City or Town: Schertz, TX.

How to get: You can reach The DoSeum by car and park in the museum's parking lot. Metropolitan Transit operates several bus routes that stop near the museum. You can also take a VIA streetcar to the Pearl District and walk to the museum.

GPS coordinates. 29.4533° N, 98.4717° W

Best Time to Visit: Throughout the year.

Pass/Permit/Fees: The ticket costs $4-$16. Kids at the age of 1 are free.

Did you know? It is a great learning place for kids.

16. Morgan's Wonderland

Morgan's Wonderland is a non-profit theme park in San Antonio, Texas, designed for individuals with special needs and their families. The park features over 25 accessible rides and attractions, including a carousel, a Ferris wheel, and a train ride. Morgan's Wonderland also offers sensory-friendly activities, such as a splash pad and a sand play area, and hosts special events and programs throughout the year. In addition to providing a fun and inclusive environment for people with disabilities, the park also serves as a center for researching and developing adaptive technologies and equipment.

Location: 5223 David Edwards Dr, San Antonio, TX 78233, USA

Closest City or Town: Schertz, TX

How to get: To reach Morgan's Wonderland, visitors can take their car and park in the free parking lot, use Metropolitan Transit buses or paratransit service, or take a taxi or ride-sharing service.

GPS coordinates. 29.5391° N, 98.3926° W

Best Time to Visit: Throughout the year.

Pass/Permit/Fees: The ticket costs $11-$17. Kids at the age of 3 are free.

Did you know? It is an inspiring destination that promotes inclusion and accessibility for all.

17. Main Plaza

Main Plaza is a historic public square in downtown San Antonio's heart. The plaza was established in the early 1700s and has served as a cultural hub for the city ever since. It is surrounded by several notable landmarks, including San Fernando Cathedral, the Bexar County Courthouse, and the Spanish Governor's Palace. Main Plaza is home to various events and festivals throughout the year, including concerts, cultural celebrations, and public art displays. Visitors can relax on the plaza's shaded benches, stroll around the fountain, or explore the nearby museums and shops that makeup San Antonio's vibrant downtown scene.

Location: San Antonio, TX 78205, USA

Closest City or Town: Schertz, TX.

How to get: To reach Main Plaza in San Antonio, TX, drive to 115 N Main Ave, or take a VIA Metropolitan Transit bus that stops nearby. Walking or biking is also an option if you're already downtown.

GPS coordinates. 29.4264° N, 98.4896° W.

Best Time to Visit: Throughout the year.

Pass/Permit/Fees: The ticket costs $11-$17. Kids at the age of 3 are free.

Did you know? The main plaza is a central gathering place and public square.

18. St Joseph Catholic Church

St. Joseph Catholic Church is a historic church in the heart of downtown San Antonia. The Church was built in the 1800s and is known for its stunning Gothic architecture.

It has been a place of worship and community for generations of Catholics in San Antonio. It plays an essential role in the city's spiritual life. St. Joseph Catholic Church offers various services and activities, including daily Mass, sacraments, prayer groups, and charitable outreach programs. Visitors to San Antonio are often drawn to the Church's beauty and history and are welcome to attend Mass or explore the grounds and interior.

Location: 623 East Commerce Street in downtown San Antonio

Closest City or Town: Universal City.

How to get: You can use the car, public transportation, or a taxi service to get to the Church.

GPS coordinates. 29.4237° N, 98.4864° W

Best Time to Visit: Throughout the year.

Pass/Permit/Fees: Free Entry

Did you know? It is in ancient churches.

19. The Shops at La Cantera

The Shops at La Cantera is a premier shopping destination in San Antonio, Texas. With over 160 stores and restaurants, this upscale open-air mall offers a unique shopping experience for visitors and locals alike. The mall's stunning architecture, featuring limestone walls and modern design elements, complements the natural beauty of the Texas Hill Country surrounding it. It is home to a diverse mix of luxury brands and popular retailers, including Nordstrom, Neiman Marcus, Apple, and H&M. The Shops at La Cantera are a must-visit destination for anyone looking for a top-notch shopping experience in San Antonio.

Location: 15900 La Cantera Pkwy Suite 6698, San Antonio, TX 78256, USA

Closest City or Town: Pleasanton, TX.

How to get: The Shops at La Cantera can be reached by car via Interstate 10 West and exit at La Cantera Parkway or by VIA Metropolitan Transit bus routes 93 and 94. Ride-hailing services are available.

GPS coordinates. 29.5922° N, 98.6153° W

Best Time to Visit: Throughout the year.

Pass/Permit/Fees: Free Entry.

Did you know? It is a fine place for shopping.

20. Lackland Air Force Base

Lackland Air Force Base is a United States Air Force Base in San Antonio, Texas. It is one of the largest military training bases in the world and is responsible for basic military training for all enlisted Air Force personnel. The base is named after Brigadier General Frank Lackland, a pioneer in military aviation. In addition to basic training, Lackland AFB also houses the Air Force Security Forces Center and the Inter-American Air Forces Academy. The base is critical in maintaining the US Air Force and its personnel and is an integral part of the San Antonio community.

Location: San Antonio, TX 78236, US

Closest City or Town: Pleasanton, TX.

How to get: Lackland Air Force Base is restricted to authorized personnel and guests. Approved visitors can get there by car via Interstate 410 West and exit at Valley Hi Drive, and take VIA Metropolitan Transit bus route 611 to reach the Visitor Center.

GPS coordinates. 29.3862° N, 98.6179° W

Best Time to Visit: Throughout the year.

Pass/Permit/Fees: Approved by authorities.

Did you know? It is one of the most extensive military bases.

22. Sea World San Antonio

SeaWorld San Antonio is a marine mammal park, oceanarium, and theme park in San Antonio, Texas. The park features a wide range of marine life, including dolphins, beluga whales, sea lions, and killer whales, as well as various rides and attractions. Visitors can enjoy thrilling roller coasters, water rides, animal shows, interactive exhibits, and educational programs. SeaWorld San Antonio is also committed to marine conservation and rehabilitation efforts and offers visitors a chance to learn about these efforts and how they can help protect marine life. The park is a popular attraction for families and animal lovers visiting San Antonio.

Location: 10500 SeaWorld Dr, San Antonio, TX 78251, USA

Closest City or Town: Live Oak.

How to get: Sea World San Antonio can be accessed by car or public transportation. VIA Metropolitan Transit offers bus service.

GPS coordinates. 29.4583° N, 98.7000° W

Best Time to Visit: Summer.

Pass/Permit/Fees: The ticket costs $56-$65. Kids under 3 are free.

Did you know? It is the home of marine mammal life.

New Braunfels

1. Gruene Historic District

The Gruene Historic District is a charming New Braunfels neighborhood known for its rich history, unique architecture, and small-town charm. The district is centered around the iconic Gruene Hall, an ancient, continually operating dance hall in Texas, which has hosted legendary musicians like Willie Nelson and George Strait. Visitors can also explore the many quaint shops, restaurants, and bed and breakfasts that line the district's streets, many of which are housed in historic buildings dating back to the 1800s. The community also features several annual events, including the Gruene Music and Wine Festival, which draws visitors nationwide.

Location: New Braunfels, TX 78130, USA

Closest City or Town: Seguin, TX.

How to get: The district is approximately 30 miles northeast of San Antonio. Visitors can use a car or public transport.

GPS coordinates. 29.7392° N, 98.1049° W

Best Time to Visit: Throughout the year.

Pass/Permit/Fees: Free Entry.

Did you know? It is an ideal place for history buffs and music lovers.

2. Landa Park

Landa Park is a beautiful recreational area in New Braunfels, known for its pristine natural beauty and wide range of activities. The park spans over 196 acres and features a variety of attractions, including picnic areas, playgrounds, hiking trails, paddle boats, and a miniature train ride. Visitors can enjoy swimming in the spring-fed Comal River or relaxing on the shores of Landa Lake. The park boasts a stunning 18-hole golf course, a miniature golf course, and a seasonal aquatic complex with several water slides and a splash pad.

Location: 164 Landa Park Dr, New Braunfels, TX 78130, USA

Closest City or Town: San Marcos, TX.

How to get: Landa Park can be accessed by car or public transportation, including local bus routes and ridesharing services.

GPS coordinates. 29.7090° N, 98.1354° W

Best Time to Visit: Summer, Spring.

Pass/Permit/Fees: Free Entry.

Did you know? The park offers activities for all ages.

3. Schlitterbahn Waterpark New Braunfels

Schlitterbahn Waterpark in New Braunfels is one of the world's largest and most popular water parks. The park spans over 70 acres and features many attractions, including water slides, lazy rivers, wave pools, and kiddie play areas. Visitors can also enjoy several on-site restaurants and shops and rent private cabanas for a more luxurious experience. The park features several unique attractions, including the world's longest water coaster, the Master Blaster, and the Falls, an artificial white water rafting course. Whether you're a thrill-seeker or simply looking for a fun day in the sun, Schlitterbahn Waterpark is a must-visit destination.

Location: 400 N Liberty Ave, New Braunfels, TX 78130, USA

Closest City or Town: Live Oak.

How to get: You can reach by car or public transportation. The shuttle service is available from downtown New Braunfels.

GPS coordinates. 29.7129° N, 98.1248° W

Best Time to Visit: Summer, Spring

Pass/Permit/Fees: $8 per hour.

Did you know? It is the world's best water park with several activities.

BOERNE

1. Cascade Caverns

Cascade Caverns is a natural wonder located in Boerne, Texas, just a short drive from San Antonio. The caverns were formed millions of years ago and offer visitors the chance to explore stunning underground chambers, marvel at crystal formations, and learn about the geology and history of the region. The tour guides are knowledgeable and passionate, and the experience suits all ages and fitness levels. Additionally, the park features several outdoor attractions, including hiking trails, picnic areas, and a gem mining experience. Whether you're a nature lover, a history buff, or simply looking for a unique adventure, Cascade Caverns is a must-visit destination in Texas.

Location: 226 Cascade Cavern, Boerne, TX 78015, USA

Closest City or Town: Canyon Lake.

How to get: It is approximately 30 miles northwest of San Antonio. Visitors can use public transportation; there is no direct bus route to the park.

GPS coordinates. 29.7637° N, 98.6803° W

Best Time to Visit: Summer, Fall

Pass/Permit/Fees: prices vary according to the tour.

Did you know? It is an ideal place for geology and history lovers.

2. Cave Without a Name

Cave Without a Name is a hidden gem located in Boerne, Texas, just a short drive from San Antonio. This underground wonder was discovered in 1939 and featured stunning stalactites, stalagmites, and other unique rock formations. Visitors can hire a guided tour of the cave, learn about its history and geology, or opt for a more adventurous wild cave tour. The park offers several outdoor activities, including hiking trails, picnic areas, and a gift shop. Whether you're a nature enthusiast, a history buff, or simply looking for a unique experience, Cave Without a Name is to be noticed.

Location:325 Kreutzberg Rd, Boerne, TX 78006, USA

Closest City or Town: Canyon Lake.

How to get: Go in your car or hire a taxi. There is no direct public transport available.

GPS coordinates. 29.8863° N, 98.6184° W

Best Time to Visit: Summer, Fall

Pass/Permit/Fees: $ 11-$20. Kids under 6 are free.

Did you know? It is a wonder historical point.

VANDERPOOL

1. Lost Maples State Natural Area

Lost Maples State Natural Area is a beautiful nature reserve in the heart of the Texas Hill Country. The park spans over 2,000 acres and is known for its stunning fall foliage, hiking trails, and diverse wildlife. Visitors can explore the park's many trails, which range in difficulty and offer spectacular views of the surrounding landscape. The park offers several picnic areas, a campground, and a visitor center with exhibits on the park's history and ecology.

Location: 37221 RM 187, Vanderpool, TX 78885, USA

Closest City or Town: Kerrville, TX.

How to get: It is 85 miles northwest of San Antonio. Visiting the park during weekdays or off-season is recommended to avoid crowds, as parking is limited during peak season.

GPS coordinates. 29.8076° N, 99.5706° W

Best Time to Visit: Spring

Pass/Permit/Fees: $6. Kids under 6 are free.

Did you know? It offers a wide range of outdoor activities.

HOUSTON

1. Minute Maid Park

Minute Maid Park is a state-of-the-art baseball stadium in downtown Houston, Texas. It is the home of the Houston Astros Major League Baseball team. The park, which opened in 2000, has a unique retractable roof that allows for year-round use and a train that runs along the left field wall in tribute to Houston's railroad history. With a seating capacity of over 40,000, Minute Maid Park has hosted numerous events, including the 2004 MLB All-Star Game and the 2017 World Series. It also features a variety of amenities for fans, including restaurants, bars, and luxury suites.

Location: 501 Crawford St, Houston, TX 77002, USA

Closest City or Town: West University Place TX.

How to get: To reach Minute Maid Park, drive and exit at Hamilton or Chartres streets, and take public transit on the METRORail.

GPS coordinates. 29.7572° N, 95.3552° W

Best Time to Visit: Throughout the year.

Pass/Permit/Fees: Ticket costs vary.

Did you know? It is a must-see for any baseball fan visiting Houston.

2. The Houston Museum of Natural Science

The Houston Museum of Natural Science is a world-renowned institution in Houston, Texas. Founded in 1909, the museum houses a massive collection of art and exhibits showcasing natural history, space exploration, and anthropology. Visitors can explore various permanent and special exhibitions, including the Burke Baker Planetarium, the Morian Hall of Paleontology, and the Wiess Energy Hall. The museum also features a butterfly center, a 3D theater, and a variety of educational programs and events. With its extensive collection and interactive exhibits, the Houston Museum of Natural Science is a must-see attraction for visitors to Houston.

Location: 5555 Hermann Park Dr, Houston, TX 77030, USA

Closest City or Town: Jacinto City, TX.

How to get: You can reach by driving and turning right on Hermann Park Drive, taking the METRORail Red Line to Hermann Park/Rice University.

GPS coordinates. 29.7221° N, 95.3896° W

Best Time to Visit: Throughout the year

Pass/Permit/Fees: $16-$25

Did you know? It is the home of scientific items.

3. Children's Museum Houston

It is a non-profit educational institution that provides children with a fun and interactive learning experience. The museum offers a variety of exhibits and activities that encourage children to learn about science, technology, engineering, art, and math (STEAM) concepts through play. Some popular shows include Kidtropolis, an interactive city where children can role-play various careers, and the EcoStation, which explores environmental conservation and sustainability. The museum also offers educational programs, events, and camps yearly. With its hands-on approach to learning, the Children's Museum Houston is a must-visit destination for families and educators looking to inspire young minds.

Location: 1500 Binz St, Houston, TX 77004, USA

Closest City or Town: Aldine, TX.

How to get: It is easily accessible by car and public transportation and located at the Museum District stop.

GPS coordinates. 29.7226° N, 95.3853° W

Best Time to Visit: Throughout the year

Pass/Permit/Fees: $14-$15.Kids under 1 are free.

Did you know? It is a perfect learning place for kids.

4. Cockrell Butterfly Center

The Cockrell Butterfly Center is a popular exhibit in Houston's Houston Museum of Natural Science. It is a three-story glass enclosure that houses a living butterfly habitat. Visitors can experience the beauty of over 2,000 fluttering butterflies worldwide in a lush, tropical environment. The exhibit also features interactive displays that educate visitors on the butterfly life cycle, behavior, and conservation efforts. The center has a rainforest conservatory, which includes exotic plants, free-flying birds, and other insects.

Location: 5555 Hermann Park Dr, Houston, TX 77030, USA

Closest City or Town: Stafford, TX

How to get: Visitors can arrive by car or public transportation (METRORail or bus).

GPS coordinates. 29.7222° N, 95.3903° W

Best Time to Visit: September.

Pass/Permit/Fees: $10-$12.

Did you know? Enjoy the butterfly habitat and interactive displays about the butterfly life cycle and conservation.

5. The Menil Collection

It is a world-renowned art museum in the Montrose neighborhood of Houston. The museum was founded by John and Dominique de Menil, avid art collectors and philanthropists. The collection includes over 17,000 works of art, including pieces from ancient civilizations, modern and contemporary art, and African and Pacific Islander art. The museum is known for its unique architecture, including several buildings interconnected by pathways and courtyards. The Menil Collection also offers a variety of educational programs, including lectures, tours, and workshops.

Location: 1533 Sul Ross St, Houston, TX 77006, USA

Closest City or Town: Aldine, TX.

How to get: It is in the Montrose neighborhood. Visitors can arrive by car or public transportation (METRORail or bus).

GPS coordinates. 29.7354° N, 95.3960° W.

Best Time to Visit: Throughout the year

Pass/Permit/Fees: Free Entry.

Did you know? It is famous worldwide for its art collection.

6. National Museum of Funeral History

It is preserving the history and heritage of the funeral industry. The museum's exhibits include a collection of funeral service vehicles, historical hearses, caskets, and displays on embalming, mourning traditions, and the history of cremation. Visitors can also explore exhibits on the funerals of presidents and celebrities, including John F. Kennedy, Elvis Presley, and Michael Jackson. The museum also houses a library and archives offering research and scholarly resources. The National Museum of Funeral History provides visitors with a fascinating and thought-provoking experience with its unique focus on the history of death and mourning practices.

Location: 415 Barren Springs Dr, Houston, TX 77090, USA

Closest City or Town: Stafford.

How to get: Visitors can take Interstate 45 North and exit West Road to get there.

GPS coordinates. 29.9895° N, 95.4307° W

Best Time to Visit: Throughout the year.

Pass/Permit/Fees: $12.

Did you know? You can observe historical funeral services here.

7. Holocaust Museum Houston

It is dedicated to educating the public about the Holocaust and ensuring human rights and dignity. The museum's exhibits include artifacts, photographs, and personal accounts from survivors and witnesses of the Holocaust, and displays on the rise of Nazi power, the persecution of Jewish and other minority groups, and the liberation of concentration camps. The museum conducts educational programs, lectures, and special events to further engage visitors in learning about this dark period of history. The Holocaust Museum Houston is a powerful reminder of the consequences of intolerance and hatred and the importance of promoting peace and justice in our world.

Location: 5401 Caroline St, Houston, TX 77004, USA

Closest City or Town: Cloverleaf, TX .

How to get: Visitors can take Highway 288 South and exit at Southmore Boulevard to get there.

GPS coordinates.29.7252° N, 95.3857° W

Best Time to Visit: Throughout the year.

Pass/Permit/Fees: $16-$22.

Did you know? It highlights the dark period of history.

8. Bayou Bend Collection and Gardens

Bayou Bend Collection and Gardens is a historic house museum and gardens located in Houston, Texas. The museum is housed in the former home of Ima Hogg, a prominent Houston philanthropist, and collector of American decorative arts. The collection includes furniture, ceramics, silver, and textiles from the 17th to the 19th century, as well as paintings and sculptures from American artists. The gardens surrounding the house cover 14 acres and feature a variety of native and exotic plants, fountains, statues, and a fish pond. Bayou Bend Collection and Gardens offers programs throughout the year.

Location: 6003 Memorial Dr, Houston, TX 77007, USA

Closest City or Town: Pasadena, TX.

How to get: Visitors can take Interstate 10 West and exit at the Washington Avenue/Rice Boulevard exit to get there.

GPS coordinates. 29.7607° N, 95.4217° W

Best Time to Visit: Throughout the year.

Pass/Permit/Fees: Ticket costs vary.

Did you know? It is famous for events, programs, and historical displays.

9. Rodeo Houston or Houston Livestock Show and Rodeo

The Houston Livestock Show and Rodeo, also known as Rodeo Houston, is an annual event held in Houston, Texas, USA. The event attracts over two million visitors annually and is one of the most vast rodeos in the world. It features rodeo competitions such as bull riding, calf roping, barrel racing, and concerts by top country music artists. The event also includes a carnival, livestock shows, and a variety of food vendors. The Houston Livestock Show and Rodeo is a non-profit organization that raises money for scholarships, educational programs, and agricultural initiatives. The event has a rich history and is integral to Texas culture.

Location: NRG Pkwy, Houston, TX 77054, US

Closest City or Town: Jinto City, TX .

How to get: The event is held at NRG Park, south of downtown Houston.

GPS coordinates.29.6845° N, 95.4105° W.

Best Time to Visit: Throughout the year.

Pass/Permit/Fees: The ticket prices vary.

Did you know? It is famous worldwide for concerts.

10. Space Centre Houston

Space Center Houston is a museum and educational center in Houston, Texas, USA. It is the official visitor center for NASA's Johnson Space Center and is dedicated to educating the public about space exploration. The museum features a variety of exhibits and artifacts, including spacesuits, spacecraft, and moon rocks. Visitors can take a tram tour of the Johnson Space Center, see astronauts training for missions, and even touch a natural moon rock. Space Center Houston also offers interactive exhibits, a theater, and educational programs for all ages.

Location: 1601 E NASA Pkwy, Houston, TX 77058, USA

Closest City or Town: Bellaire, TX.

How to get: You can use the NASA Parkway to get there.

GPS coordinates. 29.5518° N, 95.0981° W

Best Time to Visit: Throughout the year.

Pass/Permit/Fees. $25-$30.

Did you know? It is a must-see destination for anyone interested in space and science.

11. Rothko Chapel

The Rothko Chapel is non-denominational in Houston, Texas, USA. It was founded by the art collectors John and Dominique de Menil and designed by the artist Mark Rothko. The chapel features 14 large-scale paintings by Rothko, displayed in a space designed to create a contemplative environment. The chapel is open to people of all faiths and is a place for meditation, prayer, and reflection. The Rothko Chapel also hosts a variety of public programs, including lectures, concerts, and interfaith events.

Location: 3900 Yupon St, Houston, TX 77006, USA

Closest City or Town: Cloverleaf, TX.

How to get: You can use roads such as US-59, I-10, and I-45 to get.

GPS coordinates. 29.7376° N, 95.3962° W

Best Time to Visit: Throughout the year.

Pass/Permit/Fees. Free Entry.

Did you know? It is a unique and significant cultural landmark.

12. Buffalo Bayou Park

Buffalo Bayou Park is a 160-acre urban park in Houston, Texas, USA. The park features numerous amenities, including hike and bike trails, a skate park, a dog park, a nature playground, and a picnic area. Visitors can rent bikes, kayaks, and stand-up paddleboards to explore the park's waterways. The park has several art installations, including the iconic "Houston" sign and the "Tolerance" sculpture. Buffalo Bayou Park is also an important conservation area that provides habitat for various wildlife species, including birds, turtles, and fish.

Location: 1800 Allen Pkwy & Memorial Dr, Houston, TX 77019, USA

Closest City or Town: Stafford, TX

How to get: You can drive and park at one of the park's several parking lots, take public transportation, bike, or walk via pedestrian

bridges such as the Rosemont, Sabine, or Jackson Hill.

GPS coordinates. 29.7621° N, 95.3974° W

Best Time to Visit: Throughout the year.

Pass/Permit/Fees. Free Entry.

Did you know? It is a home of wildlife and outdoor activities.

13. Museum of Fine Arts, Houston

The Museum of Fine Arts, Houston (MFAH) is a renowned art museum in the heart of Houston, Texas, USA. The museum's collection includes over 70,000 works, ranging from ancient to contemporary, particularly on European, American, and Latin American art. The MFAH is home to several world-class collections, including the Glassell Collection of American Art, the Rienzi Collection of European Decorative Arts, and the Ting Tsung and Wei Fong Chao Arts of China Gallery. The museum also hosts numerous exhibitions, events, and educational programs annually.

Location: 1001 Bissonnet St, Houston, TX 77005, US

Closest City or Town: Stafford, TX.

How to get it: You can use 1144 Binz Street.

GPS coordinates. 29.7256° N, 95.3905° W

Best Time to Visit: Summer.

Pass/Permit/Fees. $12-$19.

Did you know? It is the best place for art lovers.

La Porte

1. San Jacinto Battleground State Historic Site

San Jacinto Battleground State Historic Site is a historic landmark in La Porte, Texas, USA, commemorating the Battle of San Jacinto on April 21, 1836, and was a decisive victory for the Texan army over the Mexican army during the Texas Revolution. The site is home to a 570-foot-tall San Jacinto Monument, the tallest war memorial in the world. Tourists can use an elevator to the top of the monument for views of the surrounding area. The park also includes a museum, a theater, and a battlefield where visitors can learn about the history of the battle and the people who fought in it.

Location: 3523 Independence Pkwy, La Porte, TX 77571, USA

Closest City or Town: California:

How to get: To get to the San Jacinto Battleground State Historic Site, take I-10 East from Houston and exit on the San Jacinto Battleground State Historic Site exit. The park is approximately 22 miles southeast of downtown Houston.

GPS coordinates. 29.7474° N, 95.0797° W

Best Time to Visit: June-August.

Pass/Permit/Fees. $5-$10.

Did you know? It is a historical landmark with a fantastic view.

KEMAH

1. Kemah Boardwalk

Kemah Boardwalk is a popular entertainment destination in Kemah, Texas, USA. Built along Galveston Bay, this 60-acre amusement park features a variety of attractions, restaurants, and shops, making it a perfect entertainment hub for families and friends to spend a day or evening. Tourists can enjoy thrilling rides such as the Boardwalk Bullet wooden roller coaster or stroll along the Boardwalk while enjoying the scenic views of the bay. The Boardwalk is also home to various restaurants serving seafood, burgers, and Tex-Mex cuisine, as well as unique shops offering souvenirs and gifts.

Location: 215 Kipp Ave, Kemah, TX 77565, USA

Closest City or Town: Seabrook. TX.

How to get: Visitors can get there by car, taxi, public transportation, or ride-sharing services.

GPS coordinates. 29.5473° N, 95.0202° W

Best Time to Visit: Summer, Fall.

Pass/Permit/Fees. Free Entry

Did you know? It is a must-visit destination for anyone visiting the Texas Gulf Coast.

BEAUMONT

1. Beaumont Botanical Gardens

Beaumont Botanical Gardens is a 23-acre public garden in the heart of Beaumont, Texas. The park offers a variety of themed gardens, including a rose garden, a cactus garden, a herb garden, and a sensory garden. Visitors can stroll along the winding pathways and admire the beautiful seasonal flowers, trees, and plants. The gardens host several events throughout the year, such as the Garden and Art Show, the Butterfly Release, and the Holiday Tree Lighting.

Location: 6088 Babe Zaharias Dr, Beaumont, TX 77705, USA

Closest City or Town: Vidor, TX.

How to get: To get to the San Jacinto Battleground State Historic Site, take I-10 East from Houston and exit on the San Jacinto Battleground State Historic Site exit. The park is approximately 22 miles southeast of downtown Houston.

GPS coordinates. 30.0242° N, 94.1462° W

Best Time to Visit: Spring

Pass/Permit/Fees. Free Entry

Did you know? It is a must-visit destination for entertainment.

GALVESTON

1. Galveston - Port Bolivar Ferry

The Port Bolivar Ferry is a free ferry service between Galveston Island and the Bolivar Peninsula in Texas, USA. The Texas Department of Transportation operates the ferry 24/7, 365 days a year. The 2.7-mile journey takes approximately 20 minutes each way and offers breathtaking views of the Gulf of Mexico and Galveston Bay. The ferry is popular among tourists and locals and is a great way to explore the Texas coastline. Visitors can also spot dolphins, pelicans, and other marine life during the crossing.

Location: 123 TX-87, Port Bolivar, TX 77650, USA

Closest City or Town: La Marque, TX.

How to get: To get to the Port Bolivar Ferry, take State Highway 87 South from Port Arthur or Highway 124 South from Winnie. Alternatively, take I-45 south from Houston and then take the exit for the Galveston-Bolivar ferry.

GPS coordinates. 29.3623° N, 94.7793° W

Best Time to Visit: Summer, Fall

Pass/Permit/Fees. Free Entry

Did you know? It is an amazing free service.

2. Bishop's Palace

Bishop's Palace is a historic home in Galveston, Texas, USA. Built in 1892 for the prominent attorney and politician Walter Gresham, the mansion was later purchased by the Roman Catholic Diocese of Galveston and used as the residence for Bishop Christopher Byrne. The building blends Victorian and Gothic architectural styles and is known for its intricate woodwork, stained glass windows, and opulent furnishings. Today, the Bishop's Palace is open to the public for guided tours, allowing visitors to explore its many rooms and learn about its fascinating history.

Location: 1402 Broadway Avenue J, Galveston, TX 77550, USA

Closest City or Town: Texas city.

How to get: To get to Bishop's Palace in Galveston, Texas, take I-45 South from Houston and exit onto Broadway Avenue. Bishop's Palace has nearby parking at the corner of 14th Street and Broadway Avenue.

GPS coordinates. 29.3031° N, 94.7822° W

Best Time to Visit: Summer

Pass/Permit/Fees. The ticket costs $5-$10. Kids under 6 are free.

Did you know? It is considered one of the top attractions in Galveston.

3. Moody Mansion

The Moody Mansion is a historic home in Galveston, Texas, USA. Built in 1895 for the wealthy entrepreneur William Lewis Moody Jr. and his family, the mansion is an excellent example of the Romanesque Revival architectural style. The house features stained glass windows, ornate carvings, and beautiful furnishings, reflecting the opulence and luxury of the Gilded Age. The Moody Mansion is open to the public for guided tours, providing visitors with a great glimpse into the life of one of Texas's most prominent families.

Location: 2618 Broadway Avenue J, Galveston, TX 77550, USA

Closest City or Town: Dickinson, TX.

How to get: To get to the Moody Mansion in Galveston, Texas, take I-45 South from Houston and exit onto Broadway Avenue. The mansion has nearby parking on the corner of 26th Street and Avenue J.

GPS coordinates. 29.2995° N, 94.7963° W

Best Time to Visit: Throughout the year.

Pass/Permit/Fees. $35 per family.

Did you know? It is famous for its culture, history, and architecture.

4. Galveston Historic Seaport - Home of the Tall Ship ELISSA

The Galveston Historic Seaport is a popular tourist destination in Galveston, Texas, USA. The seaport is home to several historic ships, including the Tall Ship Elissa, a three-masted, iron-hulled sailing ship built in 1877. Visitors can find the boat and learn about its fascinating history, which includes more than a century of service as a cargo ship and a restoration in the 1970s. The seaport also offers a variety of other attractions, including waterfront dining, shopping, and fishing charters.

Location: Pier 22 Suite, 8, Galveston, TX 77550, USA

Closest City or Town: League City.

How to get: To get to the Galveston Historic Seaport in Texas, take I-45 South from Houston and exit onto Harborside Drive. Follow Harborside Drive until you reach 22nd Street and the seaport at the end of 22nd Street.

GPS coordinates. 29.3091° N, 94.7933° W

Best Time to Visit: Throughout the year.

Pass/Permit/Fees. $7-$10.

Did you know? It is perfect for anyone interested in maritime history.

5. Galveston Naval Museum

The Galveston Naval Museum is located on the historic Seawall Boulevard in Galveston, Texas, and is home to several fascinating exhibits related to the United States naval history. The museum showcases a range of maritime artifacts, including an extensive collection of model ships, vintage uniforms, and weaponry. One of the museum's main attractions is the USS Cavalla, a World War II submarine that significantly sank the Japanese aircraft carrier Shokaku. Visitors to the museum can also tour the USS Stewart, a destroyer escort that served in World War II and the Korean War.

Location: 100 Seawolf Park Blvd, Galveston, TX 77554, USA

Closest City or Town: League City.

How to get: It is easily accessible by car or public transportation.

GPS coordinates. 29.3345° N, 94.7794° W

Best Time to Visit: Throughout the year.

Pass/Permit/Fees. $13.

Did you know? It is a perfect place for history buffs.

6. Ocean Star Offshore Drilling Rig & Museum

The Ocean Star Offshore Drilling Rig & Museum is in Galveston and is for the history and technology of offshore oil drilling. The museum is a home of a retired offshore drilling rig that was in operation from 1969 to 1984, providing visitors with a unique opportunity to see how drilling operations were conducted during that era. The museum hosts a range of exhibits, including models of offshore drilling platforms, interactive displays, and videos detailing the history and science of offshore drilling. Visitors can also climb aboard the drilling rig and explore the living quarters, drill floor, and other platform areas.

Location: 2002 Wharf Rd, Galveston, TX 77550, USA

Closest City or Town: Alvin TX.

How to get: It is easily accessible by car or public transportation.

GPS coordinates. 29.3104° N, 94.7917° W

Best Time to Visit: Throughout the year.

Pass/Permit/Fees. $6-S10. Kids under 6 are free.

Did you know? It is famous for its energy industry and history.

7. Galveston's St. Street Fishing Pier

Galveston's 61st Street Fishing Pier is a must-visit attraction for fishing enthusiasts in Texas. Spanning over the Gulf of Mexico, this pier has all the gear and supplies needed for a successful fishing trip. Anglers can expect to catch fish like redfish, speckled trout, and flounder. Additionally, the pier features a restaurant and bar that offers visitors a wide range of refreshments and dining options. The pier's picturesque view of the ocean and Galveston Island makes it an ideal place to relax and enjoy the serenity of the Gulf.

Location: 6101 Seawall Blvd, Galveston, TX 77551, USA

Closest City or Town: Webster TX.

How to get: It is easily accessible by car or public transportation, with ample parking and a convenient location.

GPS coordinates. 29.2649° N, 94.8252° W

Best Time to Visit: Throughout the year.

Pass/Permit/Fees. $12

Did you know? It is famous for fun and adventure.

8. Tree Sculptures

The tree sculptures of Galveston, Texas, are a unique and remarkable attraction that showcases the talent of local artists. The sculptures were created from trees damaged during Hurricane Ike in 2008 and transformed into beautiful works depicting everything from marine life to historical figures. Visitors can use a self-guided tour of the sculptures throughout the city, with many of them located in public parks and other outdoor spaces. The sculptures have become an integral part of

Galveston's cultural landscape, and their preservation and continued creation have become a source of pride for the city and its residents.

Location: 14603 Fonmeadow Dr, Houston, TX 77035, USA

Closest City or Town: Alvin TX.

How to get: Visitors can take a self-guided tour using a map or join a guided tour for a more in-depth experience.

GPS coordinates. 29.6378° N, 95.5069° W

Best Time to Visit: Summer, Spring.

Pass/Permit/Fees. $25-50.

Did you know? It is a unique place to visit.

9. Schlitterbahn Waterpark Galveston

Schlitterbahn Waterpark in Galveston, Texas, is an exciting destination for water lovers of all ages. The park features over 30 water attractions, including thrilling water slides, lazy rivers, and wave pools. Visitors can also relax in the park's many lounging areas or grab a bite at one of its many restaurants. For the ultimate experience, visitors can rent a private cabana or reserve a group party room. Schlitterbahn Waterpark is open seasonally from March to September, making it the perfect summer destination for families and anyone looking to beat the Texas heat.

Location: 2109 Gene Lucas Blvd, Galveston, TX 77554, USA

Closest City or Town: Webster TX.

How to get: Visitors can reach by taking Exit 1C toward Harborside Drive from Interstate 45 South, following Harborside Drive to 25th Street.

GPS coordinates. 29.2704° N, 94.8517° W

Best Time to Visit: March-September.

Pass/Permit/Fees. $40.

Did you know? It is famous for fun and water activities.

MATAGORDA

1. Matagorda Bay Nature Park

Matagorda Bay Nature Park is a picturesque destination on the Gulf Coast of Texas. The park is known for its beautiful beaches, scenic views, and abundant wildlife, including dolphins, pelicans, and sea turtles. Visitors can enjoy various outdoor activities, including fishing, hiking, bird watching, and kayaking. The park also features camping facilities, with both primitive and RV campsites available. For those seeking a unique experience, the park offers guided night-time beach walks during sea turtle nesting season.

Location: 6430 FM Rd 2031, Matagorda, TX 77457, USA

Closest City or Town: Bay City, TX.

How to get: You can reach by taking US-59 S toward Victoria, then turning onto TX-35 S and following FM2031 for approximately 8 miles to the park entrance.

GPS coordinates. 28.6010° N, 95.9774° W

Best Time to Visit: Throughout the year.

Pass/Permit/Fees. $9-$14.

Did you know? It is the best place to experience the natural beauty of the Texas Gulf Coast.

CORPUS CHRISTI

1. USS Lexington Museum

The USS Lexington Museum is a fascinating attraction in Corpus Christi, Texas. The museum is built on board the USS Lexington, a World War II-era aircraft carrier decommissioned in 1991 and turned into a museum. The ship served in several battles during the war and was nicknamed "The Blue Ghost" due to its ability to evade enemy attacks. Visitors can visit the boat and learn about its history through various exhibits and displays. The museum features interactive exhibits, flight simulators, and a 3D theater. Visitors can also walk through the ship's different decks and compartments, including the engine room, bridge, and flight deck.

Location: 2914 N Shoreline Blvd, Corpus Christi, TX 78402, USA

Closest City or Town: Portland, TX.

How to get: You can reach the shore of Corpus Christi Bay at 2914 N. Shoreline Blvd,

easily accessible by car, public transport, or taxi/rideshare.

GPS coordinates. 27.8151° N, 97.3887° W.

Best Time to Visit: Throughout the year.

Pass/Permit/Fees. $15-$19. Kids under 4 are free.

Did you know? It is an educational and memorable experience for all ages.

2. Padre Island National Seashore

Padre Island National Seashore is a stunning natural wonder located off the coast of southern Texas. It is the world's most extensive stretch of undeveloped barrier island, over 70 miles. The seashore is famous for its diverse range of wildlife, such as sea turtles, dolphins, and over 380 species of birds.

Visitors to the park can enjoy various outdoor activities, including beachcombing, camping, hiking, and fishing. The park also offers ranger-led programs and educational exhibits that provide insight into the area's rich natural and cultural history.

Location: Texas, USA.

Closest City or Town: Alice, TX.

How to get: Drive to Corpus Christi and take Highway 358 to the Padre Island Causeway, the only road leading to the national seashore. The park is open year-round and accessible by car, RV, and shuttle services from nearby cities.

GPS coordinates. 27.0855° N, 97.3841° W

Best Time to Visit: Spring, Fall.

Pass/Permit/Fees. Different packages are available.

Did you know? It is famous for its relaxing and peaceful environment.

3. Malaquite Beach

Malaquite Beach is a picturesque stretch of coastline within the Padre Island National Seashore in southern Texas. The beach is famous for its powdery white sand, crystal clear waters, and abundant wildlife, making it a destination for nature lovers and beachgoers. Visitors to Malaquite Beach can enjoy various outdoor activities, including swimming, sunbathing, fishing, and viewing wildlife. The beach is a fabulous spot for camping, with several campsites just a short walk from the water's edge. Malaquite Beach is a beautiful and relaxing destination that offers something for everyone.

Location: FPGG+XH, Corpus Christi, TX 78418, USA

Closest City or Town: Rockport, TX .

How to get: You can access it by car, RV, or shuttle services. Follow the signs to the beach on the park's northern end, about 23 miles from the entrance, with ample parking available.

GPS coordinates. 27.4775° N, 97.2735° W

Best Time to Visit: Spring, Summer.

Pass/Permit/Fees. Free Entry.

Did you know? It is the best place to feel nature's beauty.

TEXAS BUCKET LIST

PORT ARANSAS

1. Port Aransas Beach

Port Aransas Beach is a popular destination located on Mustang Island, just off the coast of Texas. The beach features miles of pristine white sand, crystal clear waters, and various outdoor activities, including swimming, fishing, surfing, and birdwatching. Port Aransas Beach is famous for its laid-back, bohemian vibe, with plenty of restaurants, shops, and galleries to explore. Visitors can enjoy fresh seafood, live music, and a variety of art and cultural events throughout the year.

Port Aransas Beach offers a perfect blend of relaxation and adventure, making it a top destination for beach lovers and nature enthusiasts.

Location: MILE MARKER 24 Aransas, TX 78373, USA, Corpus Christi, TX, US

Closest City or Town: Robstown, TX.

How to get: Travel to Mustang Island via the JFK Causeway from Corpus Christi or by ferry from Aransas Pass. Once on the island, follow the signs to the beach, where ample parking is available.

GPS coordinates. 27.8274° N, 97.0530° W

Best Time to Visit: Spring, Summer

Pass/Permit/Fees. Free Entry.

Did you know? It is a famous place for hang-out.

2. Leonabelle Turnbull Birding Center

The Leonabelle Turnbull Birding Center is a must-visit destination for bird enthusiasts visiting the Rockport-Fulton area of Texas. The center is located on the shores of Little Bay and provides a unique opportunity to observe various coastal birds, including herons, egrets, pelicans, and ducks.

The center features a raised boardwalk that meanders through the wetlands, giving visitors a close-up look at the birds and other wildlife in their natural habitat. The gallery also offers stunning views of the bay and the surrounding landscape, making it an excellent spot for photography and nature observation.

Location: 1356 Ross Ave, Port Aransas, TX 78373, USA

Closest City or Town: Rockport, TX.

How to get: Travel to Rockport, Texas, and head north a few miles to the center, located on the shores of Little Bay.

GPS coordinates. 28.0266° N, 97.0494° W

Best Time to Visit: Fall, Summer.

Pass/Permit/Fees. Free Entry.

Did you know? It is a peaceful and serene destination of natural beauty.

BROWNSVILLE

1. Boca Chica State Park

Boca Chica State Park is a 1,100-acre park in southern Texas. The park boasts beautiful beaches, dunes, and wetlands, making it a popular destination for birdwatching, fishing, and beachcombing. Visitors can also enjoy hiking and biking trails that wind through the park's diverse landscapes. Boca Chica State Park is also known for its role in space exploration. The park is adjacent to the SpaceX launch site, where the company is testing and launching rockets as part of its mission to send humans to Mars eventually. Visitors to the park can sometimes glimpse these rockets being tested or launched.

Location: Boca Chica Blvd, Brownsville, TX 78521, USA

Closest City or Town: San Benito, TX.

How to get: Visitors can take Highway 48, east of Brownsville, Texas. The park entrance is at the end of the highway, just before reaching the Gulf of Mexico.

GPS coordinates. 26.0042° N, 97.1944° W

Best Time to Visit: Throughout the year

Pass/Permit/Fees. Free Entry.

Did you know? It is famous for enjoying nature.

2. Gladys Porter Zoo

Gladys Porter Zoo is a 31-acre zoo in Brownsville, Texas, USA. The zoo is the house of over 1,500 animals representing 400 species worldwide. Visitors can see a wide range of animals, including lions, tigers, giraffes, zebras, and many species of birds and reptiles. Gladys Porter Zoo offers educational programs and interactive experiences for visitors of all ages. The zoo also features a children's play area, a gift shop, and a restaurant.

Gladys Porter Zoo is dedicated to conservation and animal welfare and promotes awareness of the importance of protecting endangered species and their habitats.

Location: 500 E Ringgold St, Brownsville, TX 78520, USA

Closest City or Town: San Benito, TX.

How to get: Visitors can access it by taking Interstate 69E or Highway 77/83 to the city. The zoo is located on Ringgold Street, just south of the intersection with Sixth Street, making it easily accessible by car.

GPS coordinates.25.9134° N, 97.4954° W

Best Time to Visit: Throughout the year.

Pass/Permit/Fees. The tickets cost $10-$ 16.Kids under 2 are free.

Did you know? It is famous for its wildlife habitat.

SOUTH PADRE

1. Island Sea Turtle, Inc

Sea Turtle, Inc is a non-profit organization on South Padre Island, Texas, USA, dedicated to rescuing and rehabilitating sea turtles. The organization was founded in 1977 and has helped thousands of sea turtles through its rescue and rehabilitation efforts. Visitors to Sea Turtle, Inc can take part in guided tours of the facility and learn about the organization's mission and the challenges that sea turtles face. The facility also features a turtle hospital, educational exhibits, and a gift shop.Sea Turtle, Inc promotes awareness of the importance of protecting sea turtles and their habitats and is committed to conserving these important marine creatures for future generations.

Location: 6617 Padre Blvd, South Padre Island, TX 78597, US

Closest City or Town: Brownsville, TX.

How to get: Visitors can access Highway 100 east from Port Isabel by car or the Island Metro's Purple or Yellow bus route.

GPS coordinates. 26.1369° N, 97.1738° W

Best Time to Visit: October - December

Pass/Permit/Fees. The tickets cost $6- $ 10.Kids under 5 are free.

Did you know? It is famous for turtle rehabilitation.

2. South Padre Island Birding and Nature Center

South Padre Island Birding and Nature Center is a 50-acre nature preserve in South Padre Island, Texas. The center is home to various birds, butterflies, and other wildlife, as well as several miles of walking trails, boardwalks, and observation decks. Visitors to the South Padre Island Birding and Nature Center can take guided tours of the preserve, visit the center's education exhibits and gift shop, and explore the many outdoor areas. The center also offers educational programs and events throughout the year. The South Padre Island Birding and Nature Center promotes conservation and preserving the natural beauty of South Padre Island for future generations.

Location: 6801 Padre Blvd, South Padre Island, TX 78597, USA

Closest City or Town: Brownsville, TX .

How to get: Visitors can access Highway 100 east from Port Isabel by car or the Island Metro's Purple or Yellow bus route.

GPS coordinates. 26.1375° N, 97.1743° W

Best Time to Visit: July-September.

Pass/Permit/Fees. The tickets cost $8- $ 10.Kids under 4 are free.

Did you know? It is a home of wildlife, insects, and birds.

DEL RIO

1. Devils River State Natural Area

Devils River State Natural Area is a pristine wilderness area in southwest Texas. It covers over 37,000 acres; the park is around the crystal-clear Devils River, widely considered one of the most pristine waterways in Texas. The area is characterized by rugged limestone canyons, abundant wildlife, and unique flora and fauna, making it a famous destination for hiking, camping, and fishing. The park is home to over 40 miles of the Devils River, offering various outdoor recreational activities, including kayaking, canoeing, and swimming. With its remote location and stunning natural beauty, Devils River State Natural Area is a must-visit for nature lovers and outdoor enthusiasts.

Location: 21715 Dolan Crk Rd, Del Rio, TX 78840, USA

Closest City or Town: Eagle Pass, TX.

How to get: The Park is approximately 70 miles north of Del Rio and 150 miles west of San Antonio. It is accessible by road.

GPS coordinates.29.9402° N, 100.9698° W

Best Time to Visit: Spring

Pass/Permit/Fees. $10

Did you know? It is an ideal place for outdoor activities.

Sonora

1. Caverns of SonoraCaverns of Sonora

The Caverns of Sonora is a natural wonder in Sonora, Texas, USA. The cave system is known for its exquisite mineral formations, including stalactites, stalagmites, helictites, and other rare speleothems. The caverns form over millions of years through the slow process of dissolved limestone deposited by dripping water. Visitors can take guided tours through the cave system, which includes well-lit walkways and underground streams. The Caverns of Sonora are also home to various unique wildlife, including cave-adapted spiders, crickets, and beetles, making it an essential destination for nature enthusiasts and cave explorers.

Location: 1711 Private Rd 4468, Sonora, TX 76950, USA

Closest City or Town: Del Rio, TX.

How to get: The Caverns of Sonora are accessible by road. Visitors can take Interstate 10 and exit at 392, then travel west for approximately 4 miles until they reach the cave entrance.

GPS coordinates.30.5551° N, 100.8122° W

Best Time to Visit: Spring

Pass/Permit/Fees. $20

Did you know? It is a home of insects and wildlife.

TERLINGUA

1. Chisos Mountains

The Chisos Mountains are a Big Bend National Park mountain range in southwestern Texas, USA. Its range is the only mountain range in the United States to contain within a national park. The Chisos Mountains are part of the Trans-Pecos region of T2.exas and are known for their scenic beauty and diverse wildlife, including black bears, mountain lions, and javelinas. The highest peak in the range is Emory Peak, 7,825 feet (2,385 m) above sea level. The Chisos Mountains also offer a variety of hiking trails, including the famous South Rim Trail, which offers breathtaking views of the surrounding landscape.

Location: Big Bend National Park, TX 79834.

Closest City or Town: Fort Davis.

How to get: Big Bend National Park is in southwestern Texas. Visitors can reach the mountains by car, air, or bus and access hiking trails from the Chisos Basin Visitor Center.

GPS coordinates.29.2700° N, 103.3000° W

Best Time to Visit: Summer, Fall

Pass/Permit/Fees. $8-$16

Did you know? It is a popular place for hiking, climbing, and traveling.

2. Ross Maxwell Scenic Drive

Ross Maxwell Scenic Drive is a breathtaking 30-mile drive that runs through the heart of Big Bend National Park in southwestern Texas—the drive winds through rugged canyons, towering cliffs, and vast desert landscapes. The road also passes by several historic sites, including the ruins of Sam Nail Ranch and Homer Wilson Ranch. Visitors can stop at several overlooks, such as Sotol Vista and Mule Ears Overlook, to take in the stunning vistas. Ross Maxwell Scenic Drive is a must-see attraction for anyone visiting Big Bend National Park and is a great way to experience the park's natural beauty.

Location: Texas 79834, USA.

Closest City or Town: Fort Davis.

How to get: Visitors must travel to Big Bend National Park, located in southwestern Texas near the border with Mexico. The scenic drive can be accessed from Panther Junction Visitor Center by car, air, or bus.

GPS coordinates. 29.1922° N, 103.2604° W

Best Time to Visit: Summer, Fall

Pass/Permit/Fees. $15

Did you know? It is famous for its historical site and natural beauty.

3. Big Bend National Park

Big Bend National Park is a vast protected area in southwestern Texas, USA, covering over 800,000 acres of land. The park is named after the big bend in the Rio Grande River, which forms a natural border between the United States and Mexico. The park is famous for its diverse range of flora and fauna, with over 1,200 species of plants and 450 species of birds. Visitors to the park can explore the Chisos Mountains and take a scenic drive along Big Bend National Park is a natural wonder and a must-see destination for any nature enthusiast.

Location: Texas 79834, USA.

Closest City or Town: Fort Davis.

How to get: Visitors can travel by car, air, or bus. The park has three entrances: the north entrance, the west entrance, and the east entrance, and visitors can explore the park's attractions.

GPS coordinates. 29.2498° N, 103.2502° W

Best Time to Visit: Spring.

Pass/Permit/Fees. $15-$55.

Did you know? It is famous for its flora, fauna, and plants.

4. Santa Elena Canyon

Santa Elena Canyon is a breathtaking natural wonder in Big Bend National Park in southwestern Texas. The canyon was formed by the Rio Grande River carving through the mountains, creating towering walls up to 1,500 feet. Visitors to the canyon can hike along the river, float down the rapids, or take in the stunning views from the canyon rim. The canyon is also home to diverse wildlife, including river otters, mountain lions, and black bears. Santa Elena Canyon is a must-

see destination for any nature lover visiting Big Bend National Park.

Location: Texas 79852, USA.

Closest City or Town: Fort Davis.

How to get: Visitors should travel to the west entrance and follow signs for Ross Maxwell Scenic Drive. From there, it is approximately 13 miles to the canyon turnoff, where visitors can park and begin their hike or guided tour.

GPS coordinates: 29.3034° N, 103.6152° W

Best Time to Visit: Spring, Summer.

Pass/Permit/Fees. $30-$55.

Did you know? It is famous for hiking, natural beauty, and wildlife.

5. Lost Mine Trail

The Lost Mine Trail is a popular Big Bend National Park hiking trail in southwestern Texas. The track is approximately 5 miles round-trip and offers stunning views of the Chisos Mountains. Hikers on the course can enjoy scenic vistas, rugged terrain, and the opportunity to spot local wildlife such as mule deer and black bears. At the end of the course, hikers reward with panoramic views of the desert landscape and the distant peaks of Mexico. The Lost Mine Trail is a must-see destination for anyone visiting Big Bend National Park who enjoys hiking and outdoor adventure.

Location: Texas 79834, USA

Closest City or Town: Fort Davis.

How to get: Visitors should travel to the Basin Visitor Center in the Chisos Basin area and take Basin Road to the trailhead. The trailhead is approximately 6 miles from the center, and the hike is about 2.5 miles round-trip.

GPS coordinates: 29.2528° N, 103.2929° W

Best Time to Visit: Spring, Summer.

Pass/Permit/Fees. $30-$55.

Did you know? It is the home of hiking.

FORT DAVIS

1. McDonald Observatory

McDonald Observatory is located in the Davis Mountains of West Texas and is operated by the University of Texas at Austin. The observatory was established in 1932 and has become one of the world's leading astronomical research facilities. The site's remote location and high altitude provide excellent optical and infrared astronomy observing conditions. The observatory's telescopes are used to make groundbreaking discoveries in various fields, including exoplanet detection and cosmology. It is open to the public, offering daily tours and stargazing events, making it a popular destination for astronomy enthusiasts and tourists.

Location: McDonald Observatory, 3640 Dark Sky Dr, Fort Davis, TX 79734, USA

Closest City or Town: Fort Davis.

How to get: To get to McDonald Observatory, take Texas State Highway 118 south from Fort Davis for 10 miles, then turn right onto Texas State Highway 17 and drive for 8 miles before turning left onto Observatory Road for 9 miles up to the observatory. The road leading up to the observatory is steep and winding, and the observatory is in a remote area with limited cell phone service, so plan your visit accordingly.

GPS coordinates: 30.6797° N, 104.0247° W

Best Time to Visit: Fall.

Pass/Permit/Fees. $3-$20.

Did you know? It is famous for astronomy.

2. Fort Davis National Historic Site

Fort Davis National Historic Site is a well-preserved frontier military post in the Davis Mountains of West Texas. It was established in 1854; the fort served as a strategic base for the US Army in protecting the region from raiding Apache Indians. Today, visitors can explore the fort's original buildings and learn about the daily life of soldiers stationed there. The site also features exhibits on the Buffalo Soldiers, African American troops who served at the fort in the late 1800s. The scenic drive to the defense is a highlight, with views of rugged mountains and expansive vistas.

Location: 1504 State St, Fort Davis, TX 79734, USA.

Closest City or Town: Fort Davis.

How to get: Visitors can take Highway 17 south from Balmorhea for approximately 24 miles until they reach the town of Fort Davis. Turn right onto Highway 118 and go south for about 4 miles until you see the entrance sign on the right-hand side of the road.

GPS coordinates: 30.5988° N, 103.8954° W

Best Time to Visit: February to July.

Pass/Permit/Fees. $35.

Did you know? It is a known place for the military and soldiers.

3. Davis Mountains State Park

Davis Mountains State Park is a 2,709-acre park in the Davis Mountains of West Texas. The park features scenic views, rugged terrain, and diverse wildlife, including mule deer, javelinas, and over 200 species of birds. Visitors can enjoy hiking, camping, birdwatching, stargazing, and more. The park's interpretive center offers exhibits on local history and ecology, ranger-led programs, and guided hikes. The park's Skyline Drive also offers stunning panoramic views of the surrounding mountains and valleys.

Location: H3V6+G93, Park Rd 3, Fort Davis, TX 79734, USA

Closest City or Town: Fort Davis.

How to get: To get to Davis Mountains State Park in Texas, take Highway 118 north from Fort Davis for approximately 4 miles until you see the entrance sign on the left-hand side of the road.

GPS coordinates: 30.5991° N, 103.9294° W

Best Time to Visit: January-June.

Pass/Permit/Fees. $6.

Did you know? It is the home of outdoor activities.

El Paso

1. Scenic Drive - Overlook

Scenic drives are a great way to explore the beauty of nature and soak in the picturesque views of landscapes. One of the most popular and breathtaking scenic drives is the Overlook Scenic Drive. It is a winding road that takes you through stunning vistas and overlooks, providing spectacular views of the natural scenery. The drive offers glimpses of the area's rugged cliffs, rolling hills, and scenic beauty. The route has plenty of pullouts and overlooks where you can stop and take in the views.

Location: Scenic Dr, El Paso, TX 79902, USA

Closest City or Town: Horizon City.

How to get: Plan your route, rent a car, or join a tour group to get to the Overlook Scenic Drive. Remember to check the weather and be prepared for any restrictions or rules.

GPS coordinates: 31.7826° N, 106.4797° W

Best Time to Visit: Summer, Spring.

Pass/Permit/Fees. Different packages available.

Did you know? It is the best place to explore natural beauty.

2. Franklin Mountains State Park

Franklin Mountains State Park is a beautiful natural park in El Paso, Texas. The park is spread over 24,000 acres and features rugged mountains, rocky canyons, and a wide variety of wildlife. It is a popular destination for hiking, mountain biking, rock climbing, and camping. The park boasts over 100 miles of hiking trails, including the challenging Ron Coleman Trail, which rewards hikers with eye-catching views of the surrounding landscape. Visitors can also explore the park's historic sites, including Native American rock art and an old mine.

Location: Tom Mays Park Access Rd, El Paso, TX 79930, USA

Closest City or Town: Horizon City.

How to get: Plan your route, rent a car, or join a tour group, and remember to check the park hours and bring the necessary supplies.

GPS coordinates: 31.9117° N, 106.5174° W

Best Time to Visit: Summer, Spring.

Pass/Permit/Fees. $5.

Did you know? The park offers multiple outdoor activities.

SALT FLAT

1. Guadalupe Peak

Guadalupe Peak is the highest peak in Texas, standing at 8,751 feet above sea level. It is in Guadalupe Mountains National Park, on the Texas-New Mexico border. The mountain offers eye-catching landscape views and is a famous destination for hikers and outdoor enthusiasts. The Guadalupe Peak Trail is a challenging 8.4-mile hike that takes visitors to the summit. Hikers can enjoy panoramic views, rocky terrain, and diverse wildlife. Guadalupe Peak is a must-visit destination for anyone looking to experience the beauty of Texas's natural landscape.

Location: Texas 79847, United States

Closest City or Town: Carlsbad.

How to get: Plan your route and rent a car from El Paso or Carlsbad, New Mexico. Check park hours, start early, bring supplies, and pay the admission fee. The hike begins at the Pine Springs Trailhead, accessible via a paved road from US-62/180.

GPS coordinates: 31.8912° N, 104.8605° W

Best Time to Visit: Summer, Fall.

Pass/Permit/Fees. $10.

Did you know? It is famous for its landscape and hiking.

AMARILLO

1. Cadillac Ranch

Cadillac Ranch is a unique art installation along Route 66 in Amarillo, Texas. It features ten brightly-painted Cadillac cars, ranging in age from 1949 to 1963, buried nose-first in the ground. Visitors are welcome to explore the installation, leave their mark with spray paint, and even bring their cans of spray paint to add to the artwork. Cadillac Ranch has become a popular destination for travelers, artists, and photographers and has been featured in several films, music videos, and advertisements.

Location: 13651 I-40 Frontage Rd, Amarillo, TX 79124, USA

Closest City or Town: Borger, TX .

How to get: Plan your route, rent a car, and follow Route 66, just west of Amarillo. Bring your spray paint to add to the artwork, and respect the installation and other visitors.

GPS coordinates: 35.1872° N, 101.9870° W

Best Time to Visit: Summer, Fall.

Pass/Permit/Fees. Free Entry.

Did you know? It is an iconic place to visit.

2. Cowgirls and Cowboys in the West

Cowgirls and cowboys are iconic figures in the history and culture of the American West. They are associated with the values of independence, courage, and hard work, and their legacy has been celebrated in books, films, and rodeos. These figures played an important role in shaping the American frontier, working as cattle herders, ranchers, and rodeo performers. Today, the cowboy and cowgirl traditions continue to inspire people across the country and worldwide.

Location: 19100 Farm to Market Rd 1258, Amarillo, TX 79118, USA

Closest City or Town: Dumas, TX .

How to get: Attend a rodeo, explore a ranch, visit a museum, or attend a festival. Many of these events and destinations can be found along iconic Western roads, such as Route 66 and the Pacific Coast Highway, offering a scenic and immersive experience.

GPS coordinates: 35.0146° N, 101.6627° W

Best Time to Visit: Summer.

Pass/Permit/Fees. $10-$20.

Did you know? If you're a fan of Western films or appreciate the enduring spirit of the American West, cowgirls and cowboys are a symbol of grit and determination that resonates with people of all ages.

3. Jack Sisemore Traveland RV Museum

The Jack Sisemore Travel and RV Museum is a unique museum in Amarillo, Texas, that showcases the evolution of recreational vehicles (RVs) in the United States. The museum features a collection of vintage RVs dating back to the 1930s, including iconic models like the Airstream and the Spartan. Visitors can explore the history of RV travel, from its early beginnings to the modern-day luxury RVs today. The museum also provides an interactive experience, with some exhibits allowing visitors to step inside and experience what it was like to travel in an RV from decades past.

Location: 14501 I-27, Amarillo, TX 79119, USA

Closest City or Town: Dumas, TX.

How to get: Visitors can reach Amarillo, Texas, by car, public transportation, or ride-sharing services. Its location near major highways makes it easily accessible to visitors.

GPS coordinates 35.1838° N, 101.9011° W.

Best Time to Visit: Throughout the year.

Pass/Permit/Fees. Free Entry.

Did you know? It is a famous place in history.

CANYON

1. Palo Duro Canyon State Park

Palo Duro Canyon State Park is a natural wonder in the Texas Panhandle. It is the second-largest canyon in the USA, with stunning geological formations, colorful rock formations, and a rich cultural history. Visitors can explore the canyon by hiking, biking, horseback riding, or driving. The park offers a variety of camping options, including primitive campsites, RV hookups, and cabins. In addition to outdoor activities, visitors can enjoy the park's amphitheater, which hosts musical "Texas" performances during summer.

Location: Canyon, TX 79015, USA

Closest City or Town: Hereford, TX.

How to get: You can drive from Amarillo via State Highway 217 or arrange a private tour from a local company. Unfortunately, there is no public transportation to the park.

GPS coordinates 34.9373° N, 101.6589° W

Best Time to Visit: Spring, Fall.

Pass/Permit/Fees. $8.

Did you know? It is an ideal place for anyone traveling to the Texas Panhandle.

2. Panhandle-Plains Historical Museum

The Panhandle-Plains Historical Museum is the largest history museum in Texas, located in Canyon, Texas. It features over 2 million artifacts that showcase the history and culture of the Texas Panhandle and surrounding areas. Exhibits include Native American artifacts, pioneer history, and shows on ranching and oil drilling. The museum also boasts a collection of artwork by renowned artists such as Georgia O'Keeffe and John Marin. Visitors can take guided tours, attend educational programs, and explore the museum's extensive library and archives. The Panhandle-Plains Historical Museum is a must-visit destination for anyone interested in the history and culture of the American West.

Location: 2503 4th Ave, Canyon, TX 79015, USA

Closest City or Town: Borger, TX.

How to get: Drive from Amarillo and follow the signs to Canyon to the Panhandle-Plains Historical Museum. The museum is about 15 miles south of Amarillo, and ample parking is available for visitors.

GPS coordinates 34°58'48"N, 101°55'1"W

Best Time to Visit: Spring, Fall, Summer.

Pass/Permit/Fees. $6- $13. Kids under 3 are free.

Did you know? It is best place to learn about the culture and history of West America.

TEXAS BUCKET LIST

PLANNING

Introduction

Welcome to the world of the 12 Zones of Texas! Texas is a vast and diverse state known for its rich history, culture, and natural beauty. To make it easier for tourists to navigate through the form and find the attractions that suit their interests, we divide it into 12 zones for the convenience of the visitors, each with unique characteristics and attractions.

Whether you are interested in exploring the state's vibrant cities, experiencing the rugged natural beauty of the mountains and deserts, or immersing yourself in Texas's rich history and culture, each zone has something to offer.

From the busy cities of Dallas and Houston to the rugged peaks of the Guadalupe Mountains, the 12 Zones of Texas provide a wide range of activities and attractions that cater the travelers. If you are fond of outdoor adventures, cultural backgrounds, or a taste of authentic Texas cuisine, the zones provide a roadmap to check your trip according to your interests and make the most of it. So let's explore the 12 Zones of Texas and discover the unique wonders that make this state a truly unforgettable destination.

1. First Zone

These cities are in Texas's northern and central regions. They are relatively close to each other, making them a convenient cluster of goals to visit when exploring this area of the state. Each city offers unique attractions and experiences, from the museums and cultural landmarks of Dallas and Fort Worth to the historic sites and outdoor recreation opportunities in Glen Rose and Granbury.

1. Dallas
2. Grapevine
3. Fort Worth
4. Arlington
5. Waxahachie
6. Glen Rose
7. Granbury
8. Hico
9. Pottsboro
10. Blodgett
11. Karnack

2. Second Zone

TEXAS BUCKET LIST

These cities are near the Texas Hill Country region, a popular travel destination in Texas due to its scenic landscapes, historic sites, and outdoor recreational opportunities. It is known for rolling hills, natural springs and rivers, and abundant wildlife. It offers a range of visitor activities, including hiking, biking, swimming, fishing, and exploring local wineries and breweries.

Many cities are along or near major highways, such as Highway 290 or Highway 71, making them easily accessible for travelers. Additionally, they all offer unique attractions and charm that make them worth visiting. For example, Fredericksburg is known for its German heritage and local wineries. At the same time, Johnson City is the birthplace of President Lyndon B. Johnson and offers a variety of historic sites and museums.

1. Austin
2. Burnet
3. Georgetown
4. Bend
5. Spicewood
6. Willow City
7. Fredericksburg
8. Johnson City
9. Dripping Springs
10. Wimberley
11. College Station

3. Third Zone

San Antonio, New Braunfels, Boerne, and Vanderpool are in the Texas Hill Country region, a popular tourist destination in Texas. This region is famous for its scenic beauty, including rolling hills, natural springs and rivers, and abundant wildlife. It offers a range of outdoor recreational activities, such as hiking, biking, swimming, and fishing, as well as cultural and historical attractions.

1. San Antonio
2. New Braunfels
3. Boerne
4. Vanderpool

4. Fourth Zone

Houston is the largest city in the Gulf Coast region. It offers diverse cultural attractions, like state-of-the-art places such as the Museum of Fine Arts, the Houston Museum of Natural Science, and the Space Center Houston. La Porte and Kemah are located southeast of Houston and are famous for outdoor recreational activities, including fishing, boating, and birdwatching. Beaumont is known for its historical and cultural attractions, including the Texas Energy Museum, while Galveston is known for its beaches, historical sites, and Moody Gardens theme park. Matagorda is a small coastal town known for its fishing and birdwatching opportunities. These cities offer visitors a range of activities and attractions, from cultural and historical landmarks to outdoor recreational activities and scenic beauty along the Gulf Coast.

1. Houston
2. La Porte
3. Kemah
4. Beaumont
5. Galveston
6. Matagorda

5. Fifth Zone

Corpus Christi and Port Aransas are in the Coastal Bend region of Texas. It is a famous tourist destination due to its beautiful beaches and rich wildlife. Corpus Christi is the largest city in the area. Visitors to various attractions, like the Texas State Aquarium, the USS Lexington Museum, and the Corpus Christi Museum of Science and History. It is also home to numerous parks and beaches, including the Padre Island National Seashore, which offers visitors 70 miles of undeveloped beachfront.

Port Aransas is a tiny coastal town on Mustang Island, known for its beautiful beaches and fishing opportunities. Visitors can enjoy various water sports and outdoor activities, including surfing, kayaking, and birdwatching. It is also home to the University of Texas Marine Science Institute, which researches marine ecosystems and offers educational programs for visitors.

1. Corpus Chris
2. Port Aransas

6. Sixth Zone

The Sixth Zone of Texas includes the cities of Brownsville and South Padre Island, located in the southernmost part of the state. Brownsville is a vibrant city rich in history and culture. It is a hub for commerce and education, the University Of Texas Rio Grande Valley being one of its prominent educational institutions. The city also has numerous museums and galleries showcasing its rich heritage and artistic offerings.

South Padre Island, on the other side, is a famous tourist destination known for its beautiful beaches and thriving nightlife. Located just off the coast of Texas, it offers visitors a wide range of water sports and outdoor activities, such as jet skiing, parasailing, and fishing. It is also home to numerous restaurants, bars, and clubs, making it a great place to unwind and have fun after a day of sun and surf.

1. Brownsville
2. South Padre Island

7. Seventh Zone

The Seventh Zone of Texas includes the city of Del Rio, which is in the southwestern part of the state. Del Rio has a rich history dating back to the 1800s and is home to numerous cultural and historical attractions. It is on the banks of the Rio Grande and is known for its scenic beauty and outdoor recreation opportunities.

1. Del Rio

8. Eighth Zone

The Eighth Zone of Texas includes the city of Sonora, which is in the western part of the state. Sonora is a small but vibrant city known for its rich history and natural beauty. It is in the heart of the Texas Hill Country, surrounded by rolling hills and scenic vistas. One of the main attractions in Sonora is the Caverns of Sonora, one of the worlds most beautiful and unique cave systems. The caverns are famous for their rare and unusual formations, including delicate helictites, colorful stalactites, and massive columns.

1. Sonora

9. Ninth Zone

The Ninth Zone of Texas includes the city of Terlingua, located in the western part of the state. Terlingua is a small but fascinating city steeped in history and culture. It is in the Chihuahuan Desert, surrounded by rugged mountains and starkly beautiful landscapes.

One of the main attractions in Terlingua is the Big Bend Ranch State Park, one of Texas's largest state parks. The park offers visitors various activities, including hiking, camping, fishing, and horseback riding. It is also home to numerous rare and endangered species, such as the Mexican black bear and the desert bighorn sheep.

1. Terlingua

10. Tenth Zone

The Tenth Zone of Texas includes the city of Fort Davis, which is in the western part of the state. Fort Davis is a historic city established in 1854 as a military outpost to protect travelers and settlers from Native American attacks. Today, the city is a hub for outdoor recreation and historical tourism, offering visitors a unique blend of adventure and heritage.

1. Fort Davis

11. Eleventh Zone

El Paso is also home to numerous attractions, including the Franklin Mountains State Park, one of the biggest urban parks in the USA, offering visitors a wide range of outdoor activities, such as hiking, mountain biking, and rock climbing. Other notable attractions in El Paso include the El Paso Museum of Art, the El Paso Zoo, and the Chamizal National Memorial.

Salt Flat, on the other hand, is a small community in the heart of the Chihuahuan Desert, known for its starkly beautiful landscapes and unique geological formations. It is home to the Guadalupe Mountains National Park, one of the most breathtaking natural areas in the United States, offering visitors a chance to explore its rugged peaks and deep canyons. Other notable attractions in Salt Flat include the Salt Basin Dunes, the largest gypsum dune field in the world, and the nearby town of Van Horn, which serves as a gateway to the area's many attractions.

1. El Paso
2. Salt Flat

12. Twelfth Zone

One of the main attractions in Amarillo is the Cadillac Ranch, a famous roadside attraction featuring a row of ten Cadillacs buried nose-down in the ground. The city is also home to numerous other points, including the Palo Duro Canyon State Park, the second-largest Canyon in the United States. It offers visitors various outdoor activities like hiking, camping, and horseback riding.

Conversely, Canyon is a small community located just south of Amarillo, known for its rich history and cultural heritage. It is home to the Panhandle-Plains Historical Museum, one of the largest history museums in Texas, featuring exhibits on the early pioneers, Native Americans, and cowboys who shaped the region. Canyon is also a gateway to the Palo Duro Canyon State Park, allowing visitors to explore this breathtaking natural wonder.

1. Amarillo
2. Canyon

Map

We have devised an interactive map that includes all destinations described in the book. You can easily plan your itinerary with this map, saving you time and effort.
Additionally, the map is compatible with Google Maps.

Scan the following QR or type in the provided link to receive it:

https://jo.my/txbucketlistform

You will receive an email with links to access the Interactive Map. If you do not see our email, please look for it in spam or another section of your inbox.

In case you have any problems, you can write us at **TexasBucketList@becrepress.com.**

Made in United States
Orlando, FL
11 December 2024